NOLO *and* USA TODAY

NOLO
YOUR LEGAL COMPANION

For more than 35 years, Nolo has been helping ordinary folks who want to answer their legal questions, create their own documents, or work with a lawyer more efficiently. Nolo.com provides quick information about wills, house buying, credit repair, starting a business—and just about anything else that's affected by the law. It's packed with free articles, legal updates, resources, and a complete catalog of Nolo books and software.

To find out about any important legal or other changes to this book's contents, sign up for our free update service at nolo.com/legalupdater or go to nolo.com/updates. And to make sure that you've got the most recent edition of this book, check Nolo's website or give us a call at 800-728-3555.

USA TODAY
The Nation's Newspaper

USA TODAY, the nation's largest circulation newspaper, was founded in 1982. It has nearly 3.9 million readers daily, making it the most widely read newspaper in the country.

USATODAY.com adds blogs, interactive graphics, games, travel resources, and trailblazing network journalism, allowing readers to comment on every story.

Stopping

Identity Theft

10 Easy Steps to Security

by Scott Mitic, CEO, TrustedID, Inc.

First Edition	FEBRUARY 2009
Editor	ILONA BRAY
Cover Design	JALEH DOANE
Book Design	SUSAN PUTNEY
Proofreading	ROBERT WELLS
Index	SONGBIRD INDEXING
Printing	DELTA PRINTING SOLUTIONS, INC.

Mitic, Scott
  Stopping identity theft : 10 easy steps to security / by Scott Mitic. -- 1st ed.
   p. cm.
  ISBN-13: 978-1-4133-0956-0 (pbk.)
  ISBN-10: 1-4133-0956-9 (pbk.)
  1. Identity theft--United States--Prevention. I. Title.
  HV6679.M58 2009
  332.024--dc22

                     2008037011

For information on bulk purchases or corporate premium sales, please contact Nolo's Special Sales Department. For academic sales or textbook adoptions, ask for Academic Sales. Call 800-955-4775 or write to Nolo, 950 Parker Street, Berkeley, CA 94710.

Acknowledgments

This book benefited greatly from the contributions of many different people. I owe a special debt of gratitude to the invaluable individuals who shared their stories of identity theft with me over the years, but especially to Mary Taylor, Joshua Woodruff, Cheryl Cade, and Heather Scott. I drew on an army of experts to contribute to the knowledge contained in these pages, and chief among them were Iain Mulholland, Chief Technology Officer of HauteSecure, Marian Merritt, Internet Safety Advocate at Symantec Corporation, John Benedict, Esq., Attorney at Law, Alison Vella, Real Estate Agent at Metropolitan Property Group, Mike Mansel, with Argo Insurance Group, and Kevin Lee, founder and principal of STAT Revenue Consulting. The team at Nolo provided support for the book from concept right through to finished product, led by my detailed, dedicated, and determined editor, Ilona Bray. And, finally, to Michelle Savage, who was instrumental in making this book possible, bringing patience, wisdom, and diligence to the entire effort.

About the Author

Scott Mitic is the founder and CEO of TrustedID, Inc., a leader in identity theft prevention. He is frequently quoted in the national U.S. media, and writes a blog on identity theft, at http://blog.trustedid. com. Mitic received his education at Georgetown University-The McDonough School of Business and at McGill University. He makes his home in the San Francisco Bay Area.

Dedication

To the TrustedID team,
in honor of their hard work
in the name of protecting customers
against identity theft.

Table of Contents

Your Companion in Identify Theft Protection

E very year, as many as 15 million Americans become victims of identity theft—one person every few seconds. (That's according to a 2007 survey by Gartner Research, www.gartner.com). Identity theft is the fastest growing crime in the United States, with estimated losses to the U.S. economy totaling $50 billion annually, according to the Federal Trade Commission (FTC). Victims come from all lifestyles and backgrounds, from soccer moms to lawyers to celebrities like Tiger Woods and Rosie O'Donnell. And identity thieves have no boundaries when it comes to choosing their targets. In fact, children and elderly people are among their favorite victims.

Finding out that your identity has been stolen can be devastating. And many people don't figure out what's happened for months or even years, during which time the thieves can run up debts, commit crimes, ruin medical records, and more—all in the victims' names. Cleaning up the mess and restoring your credit can take thousands of dollars and hundreds of hours to complete.

I became interested in identity theft the way most people do: It happened in my family. Then, a year later, it happened again—and it was even worse. The thief cleaned out our checking account, using our account number and a fake ID. After the second laborious process of filing a police report and making endless phone calls to our bank, I realized that I needed to get more aggressive about protecting myself and my family. I was already protecting all of our other important assets—health, home, and finances—why not our identities, too?

What started out as an individual quest for protection eventually evolved into a business, TrustedID, which helps people prevent identity theft or recover from it. Over the years, I've studied the crime inside and out. I've listened to countless people recount their personal experiences with identity theft. Some of them are short and painless, others long and torturous. Over time, the stories have changed, as the form of the crime itself has morphed to become more sophisticated and costly. Nonetheless, in many of these cases, a few simple steps could have dramatically reduced the risk of the crime occurring in the first place.

This book shows you how to take effective steps to protect yourself and your family. Keeping your identity safe requires that you be proactive in the way you approach shopping, banking, Web surfing, and just about everything else you do. But if you just learn some simple rules for guarding your most critical personal information, checking your credit report regularly, and using technology to your advantage, you'll have gone a long way to insure that you have limited—and, I hope, prevented—the damage an identity thief could do.

And if you do find that a thief has stolen your identity—or the identity of a family member—we'll show you quick action can minimize the damage and restore your privacy and your good name.

Let's get started! ●

Identity Theft— What's the Problem?

What is identity theft? It all begins when a thief steals your critical personal information for financial or personal gain. For example, thieves might use your name to:

- open new credit card accounts, then in some cases fail to pay the bills, so the delinquency gets reported on your credit record

- set up phone service

- open bank accounts and write bad checks on the account

- counterfeit checks or debit cards and drain your bank account

- take out loans to buy cars or other big-ticket items

- go shopping with your credit card

- sell your identity to other criminals or undocumented immigrants who need a clean record

- get health care (leading to confusion next time you go to the doctor), or

- shift responsibility for crimes they commit.

A thief who got away with all of these would hardly leave an area of your life untouched. But it doesn't have to go that far. The key is awareness. In this and later chapters, we'll increase your understanding of identity theft—how it occurs and how to reduce the risk—and arm you with the information you need to start protecting yourself and your family.

USA TODAY Snapshots®

How identity is stolen

The Internet, it turns out, is not the most likely source of identity theft. How identity was stolen, top responses:

Lost/stolen wallet, checkbook or credit card **38%**

Friends/acquaintances/relatives or home employees **15%**

In-store, mail, telephone purchases or transactions **15%**

Stolen paper mail **9%**

Internet **4%**

Source: Javelin Strategy & Research survey of 5,006 respondents. Margin of error: ±1 percentage points.

By Jae Yang and Karl Gelles, USA TODAY 2007

Who Commits Identity Theft?

Although many identity thieves are strangers to their victims, a fair number—and probably more than get reported—are not. Here's a fairly typical (and true) scenario: John, a salesman, already sensed something must be wrong when the phone rang early on a Saturday morning. Sure enough, it was the police, who'd arrested a man trying to use John's driver's license as identification. John immediately knew who this man was—his former neighbor, Charles.

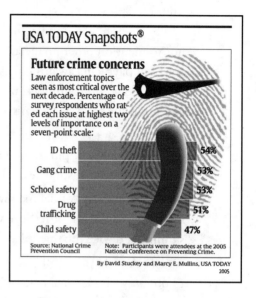

Charles and John had been next-door neighbors for three years. They'd attended the same neighborhood events and taken each other's mail in when it was time for a vacation. When Charles moved away, John was sad to see him go—until he found out six months later that Charles had used John's identity to open up two department store credit cards and take out a motorcycle loan. By the time John received the call from the police, he'd spent about 80 hours trying to clean up the damage that Charles had done—and would spend many more hours still, fending off creditors.

How Thieves Get Your Personal Information

The first reaction most people have when they find out they've become a victim of identity theft is, "But where on earth did they get my information?" In most cases, the thieves didn't have to look too hard for it. Here are just a few of their many sources:

- **Your trash.** Identity thieves go through people's trash looking for tossed financial statements, preapproved credit offers, and any other personal information. Some just pull up a car in front of someone's house, grab the recycle bin, and drive off.

- **Your mail (incoming and outgoing).** A thief who can access your mailbox before you do may find preapproved credit card offers, not to mention other financial and personal information. And your bill payments awaiting pickup, which might contain your credit card account numbers or a check you've written, are an easy and tempting mark for identity thieves.

- **Your wallet or purse.** Scammers may steal personal information from your wallet or purse, such as your credit cards, driver's license, or health insurance cards.

- **An ATM machine.** A thief may watch you enter your PIN and later steal your card, or retrieve your account information from a skimming device the thief placed on the card reader.

- **Online.** A wide variety of scams are employed by identity thieves to obtain your personal data online. In one of the most popular ones, fraudsters send "phishing" email messages designed to lure you to phony websites and reveal your personal information.

- **Shops and restaurants.** Dishonest employees steal your credit card information when you make a purchase by writing it down or using a handheld skimming device that captures your card data.

- **Databases.** Thieves can hack into corporate databases, where your personal information is stored, or buy your information on the secondary market for consumer data.

What a Thief Can Find in Your Mailbox Alone

Organizing and protecting financial statements and other documents you receive is crucial to preventing identity theft. If you don't have a secure mailbox—that is, one that's either locked or delivers mail directly into your house, beyond reach—consider getting one. Otherwise, here's a reminder of how thieves might use the information they find:

Document type	Information it may reveal	How thieves can misuse it
Credit card statements	Your name, address, creditor's name, account number, account details	To shop online or on the phone, or even change the address to which your statements are sent
Paycheck stubs	Your name, address, pay rate, employer details, and possibly your Social Security number	To apply for new credit and other accounts, especially if they have your Social Security number
New checks	Your name, address, bank's name, account number, balance, and possibly phone number or Social Security number	To write checks in your name, or access and drain your account
Bank statements	Your name, address, bank's name, account number, balance	To access your bank records and potentially drain your accounts
Investment statements	Your name, address, account number, balance, account manager, Social Security number	To apply for new accounts, especially if they have your Social Security number
Preapproved credit card offers	Your name, address, and the offer being extended to you	To change the address the company has on record for you to their address or P.O. box and then apply for the card

Which Bits of Personal Data Thieves Like Best

Without a doubt, the most precious bit of personal information to any identity thief is a Social Security number (SSN), in combination with a person's name. These two bits of data alone are enough for an identity thief to open new lines of credit, buy expensive merchandise, apply for jobs under a new name, steal money from bank accounts, and more.

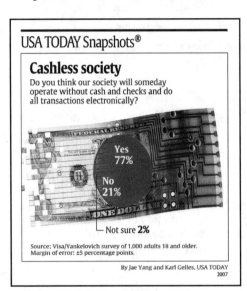

USA TODAY Snapshots®

Cashless society
Do you think our society will someday operate without cash and checks and do all transactions electronically?

Yes 77%
No 21%
Not sure 2%

Source: Visa/Yankelovich survey of 1,000 adults 18 and older. Margin of error: ±5 percentage points.

By Jae Yang and Karl Gelles, USA TODAY 2007

Take the case of Taylor, a New York City grandmother. She received letters from two collection agencies stating that she owed thousands of dollars to T-Mobile and AT&T for cell phone charges. She'd never owned a cell phone. Inquiries to both phone companies and collection agencies revealed that someone had used her name and SSN—plus an incorrect birth date—to open fraudulent accounts.

Taylor is not alone. In a highly publicized case, Michelle, an international banker, was hit hard by identity theft when a thief used her name and SSN to buy over $50,000 worth of goods and services—including a car, phone service, lines of credit, and even liposuction. Michelle later found out that there was a warrant out for her arrest in Texas for drug smuggling.

Still, many people enter their SSN on business or retail forms and applications without a second thought. It's the most frequently used record-keeping number in the United States (despite the fact that it was never intended for this purpose). The SSN is used for employee files, medical records, health insurance accounts, credit and banking accounts, student identification cards, and much more. That makes it easy for criminals to both obtain your SSN and then to use it to access your financial accounts, government records, and more.

Many people mistakenly believe that they must provide their SSN when a government agency or private business asks for it. This is not true. Select government agencies, such as motor vehicle departments, tax departments and welfare departments, can legally require your SSN. Also, banks, brokerages, and employers may have a legitimate need for it (mostly to do with tax reporting). But for the most part, other businesses and retailers have no legal right to ask for your SSN, and you shouldn't provide it unless absolutely necessary.

What about other pieces of your personal profile? Let's do a quick overview of what pieces of information need the greatest protection. Your first task will be to get familiar with this list and start practicing a "need-to-know" approach to safeguarding your sensitive personal information.

When Will You Find Out?

Many people don't discover that they've become a victim of identity theft until months later, when they're unexpectedly turned down for a loan or insurance, or get a call from a collection agency about an account they never opened. Some even get a call from the police about a crime they didn't commit.

The situation is even worse for children and the elderly, who have far less interaction with the financial world. A thief could steal the identity of a child, for example, and not be discovered until the child turns 18 and applies for his or her first credit card or student loan. (We'll discuss the details of child- and elder-identity theft in Chapter 9.)

USA TODAY Snapshots®

Most believe e-crime will increase

A vast majority of security officials believe e-crime will grow this year vs. 2004:

Increase 88%

Not sure 7%

Remain the same 4%

Decrease 1%

Source: CSO magazine, U.S. Secret Service and CERT Coordination Center survey of 819 respondents. Margin of error ±3 percentage points.

By Darryl Haralson and Adrienne Lewis, USA TODAY 2005

The later you discover identity theft, the harder—and more expensive—it is to cure. A few victims go to prison for crimes they didn't commit. And some face serious medical risks when thieves use their identity to get medical help, after doctors add a thief's medical history to their case file.

Worst Case Scenarios—Could They Happen to You?

What's the worst thing you can imagine could happen to you if your identity were stolen? Getting turned down for a loan or job because of supposed bad credit? Being rushed to the emergency room and given the wrong type of blood because someone else piggybacked on your health coverage? Getting arrested for a crime you didn't commit? All dire-sounding scenarios, but could they really happen to you?

USA TODAY Snapshots®

Identity theft raises fears

How much has Congress done to protect consumers' financial data and credit card numbers?

Too little — 75%
Just enough — 18%
Too much — 3%
Don't know — 4%

Source: iQ Research and Consulting for Adobe and RSA Security survey of 400 respondents. Margin of error ±5 percentage points.

By Jae Yang and Web Bryant, USA TODAY 2005

Unfortunately, the descriptions of identity theft cases one hears reported every day show that the worst can happen to anyone. You don't have to act recklessly or stupidly to become a victim (though it can certainly make matters worse). Here are just a few examples:

- **A thief used the identity of a major company's president to conduct international drug deals.** One morning, the president was awakened by law enforcement officials in his bedroom, who tried to arrest him at gunpoint. He eventually proved that he was not a drug dealer, but only after quite a bit of trauma.

- A graduate student was mugged in her apartment parking lot and gave up her purse, which contained her driver's license, several credit cards, and Social Security card. About 90 days later, she found out that someone had opened credit card accounts at Macy's, Mervyn's, and the Gap.

- A man thought he'd found everlasting love in his new bride, until he found out she'd used his Social Security number to open several lines of credit. Years later, he's divorced and still trying to keep the debt collectors at bay.

- A single mother was arrested in front of her children for supposedly having given birth to and abandoned a drug-addicted baby. To clear her name, she had to prove that someone else had given the hospital her name when giving birth.

- A federal prosecutor who'd put hundreds of identity thieves behind bars found out she'd been victimized when thousands of dollars disappeared from her checking account. Her information had been stolen from a medical facility database.

As you'll learn in this book, personal vigilance isn't always enough. Even if you guard your private information like a Secret Service agent protecting the president, you can't do much about problems like lackadaisical credit industry policies, the careless security practices of certain companies, and ineffective privacy laws. But there is a lot you can do.

You Can Protect Yourself—Here's How

Identity theft is a little like cancer or heart disease. While nothing can guarantee you won't get it, you can definitely raise your odds of long-term success by prevention and early detection. And a number of highly effective preventive and diagnostic steps are in fact available. Here's an outline of the steps you'll learn about in the upcoming chapters:

STEP 1: Know thy credit report. One of the most important things you can do is to order copies of your credit report at least once a year and check it for signs that someone has been taking out credit in your name.

STEP 2: Keep prying eyes off your financial accounts. Any time you pay for something, whether by credit card, debit card, cash, or check, you risk exposing your personal information. Simply understanding the types of risks involved goes a long way toward protecting you. We'll advise you on the safest methods of payment, and how to guard yourself in each transaction.

STEP 3: Be on guard when you're online. Malicious viruses, spyware, Trojan horses, worms, and other online threats can follow your movements, lurk behind the websites you visit, and ultimately steal or con you out of your personal information. You can fight back, using both technology and common sense.

STEP 4: Spot the scams before they spot you. Ever gotten an email from Nigeria asking for help transferring money out of the country? This is just one of many common identity theft scams. By learning their distinctive features, you'll avoid falling for the currently known scams, and be better able to recognize the next ones to come along.

STEP 5: Be a savvy shopper. Learn and compare the risks associated with online and offline shopping, and make sure your personal and financial information is safe no matter where or how you shop.

STEP 6: Take your personal information off the market. There's a secondary market in trading people's personal information—your Social Security number included. While you can't get off every list, you can at least limit the trading in your name.

STEP 7: Clamp down on thefts of your medical coverage. Medical identity theft, in which criminals use your personal information to obtain insurance money, prescription drugs, or medical services, can leave you stuck with medical bills that aren't yours or—even worse—an inaccurate medical chart. We'll show you how to keep this from happening to you.

STEP 8:Watch your family's back. If you have children or elders in your family who won't read this book, it may be up to you to protect them. We'll explain how they're particularly vulnerable to identity theft, and what you can do to keep thieves from abusing their clean credit and good names.

STEP 9:Have a safe trip. Planning some traveling? Learn what you can do before, during, and after your vacation or business trip to ensure that you don't fall prey to an overseas scam or come home to identity theft.

STEP 10:React quickly if your identity is stolen. The next best thing to preventing the theft of your identity is stopping it in its tracks. We'll give you a systematic rundown of what to do after discovering a theft and how to prevent and detect further harm.

USA TODAY Snapshots®

Weakest link in securing cyberspace:

| Consumers 30% | Private sector 11% | U.S. government 7% | All are equally responsible 49% | Not sure 3% |

Source: CSO magazine survey of 389 chief security officers and security executives. Margin of error ±5 percentage points.

By Jae Yang and Bob Laird, USA TODAY
2005

Know Thy Credit Report

For many people, the first sign that they've become victims of identity theft shows up in reports of their credit history. For example:

- A woman getting ready to buy a house checks her credit report and is shocked to find lists of delinquent credit accounts that she'd never opened. She is told she'll have to pay off these charges before qualifying for the mortgage.

- A man checks his report and discovers that a credit card he paid off years ago has been reopened and is carrying a large balance.

- Another man's credit report shows that someone in another state has used his name and Social Security number to open two new credit accounts.

Have you checked your credit report recently? If not, now's a great time to do so, and not only for identity-theft reasons. Everything in that report can have a major impact on your life. It tells creditors and others whether or not you pay your bills on time, have filed for bankruptcy, or have an outstanding court judgment against you. If there's something negative in the report—which there easily could be due to mere errors—you might be turned down for a credit card, a mortgage, a job, an apartment, or insurance. Even if you aren't turned down, any negative items could increase the interest rate or premium you have to pay for a loan or insurance.

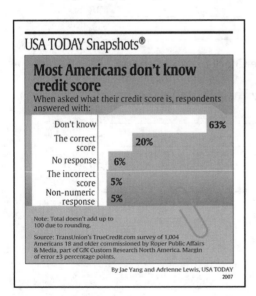

USA TODAY Snapshots®

Most Americans don't know credit score

When asked what their credit score is, respondents answered with:

Don't know	63%
The correct score	20%
No response	6%
The incorrect score	5%
Non-numeric response	5%

Note: Total doesn't add up to 100 due to rounding.

Source: TransUnion's TrueCredit.com survey of 1,004 Americans 18 and older commissioned by Roper Public Affairs & Media, part of GfK Custom Research North America. Margin of error ±3 percentage points.

By Jae Yang and Adrienne Lewis, USA TODAY 2007

That's why it's important to get up close and personal with your credit report, checking it at least once a year. This chapter will help you order and understand your credit report, look for erroneous information, spot signs of identity theft, and right any wrongs.

Your Credit Report: What It Is and Why It Matters

Credit reports are a gold mine of information about how you deal with money, not to mention related information like where you've lived and worked. Who creates these gold mines? Three major credit-reporting agencies (CRAs): Equifax, Experian, and TransUnion. They gather your information from stores, lenders, landlords, and others, compile it into a report, issue a credit score based on the data, and then sell these to virtually anyone wanting to evaluate your creditworthiness.

USA TODAY Snapshots®

States with highest credit scores

Credit scores are based on financial behavior (debt, credit usage, whether people pay bills on time, etc.). The average credit score for people in the USA is 676 (out of a possible 830). States with the highest average scores (as of January):

South Dakota	710
Vermont	707
Minnesota	706
North Dakota	705
New Hampshire	704
Massachusetts	703

Source: Experian (www.NationalScoreIndex.com)

By Shannon Reilly and Marcy E. Mullins, USA TODAY 2005

Each of us actually has three different credit reports, one from each CRA. Theoretically, each report should contain the same information and arrive at the same score. In reality, however, you may find significant differences between your three reports and scores—for example, one CRA simply may not have received notification from a lender that a new credit card account was opened in your name.

Unfortunately, neither the CRAs nor any lender checking your file make any efforts to spot errors. They'll assume you're responsible for any problems and, particularly in the case of lenders, make their decisions accordingly. In fact, some lenders (mortgage companies, for example), will look at all three scores in determining your credit risk, so one small inaccuracy could drag down your average. Credit card companies typically look at just one.

So it's up to you to review your reports—all three of them—regularly, to check for suspicious activity, and then act quickly to right any wrongs. These actions will not only help foil identity thieves, but ensure that your credit history and score put you in the best possible light with lenders and others.

How Your Score Can Change Your Life

To get an idea of how your credit score impacts your life (and your piggybank), take a look at how it determines interest rates and corresponding monthly payments on a 36-month, $25,000, new-car loan:

Score	Interest rate	Monthly Payment
720–850	6%	$761
690–719	7.4%	$777
660–689	8.5%	$789
625–659	10.8%	$816
590–624	14.3%	$858
500–589	15%	$867

SOURCE: Fair Isaac (2008 figures). To run your own numbers, go to www.myfico.com, scroll to the bottom of the page, and click "site map," then, under "Calculators," click "FICO Loan Savings Calculator." And for tips on getting your financial life together and raising your credit score, see not only the www.myfico.com website, but the book *Credit Repair*, by Robin Leonard and John Lamb (Nolo).

TIP

Don't obsess over your credit score. When you order a credit report, you'll be offered the option to see your credit score for an additional fee. While checking your score may be helpful when making a major purchase like a house or car, it's not necessary for purposes like checking whether you've become the victim of identity theft. Besides, the scores change constantly, based on the information in your credit report. If you check your score on June 1, it's likely to be different by July 1. So save your time and money—and focus on the information behind the score.

The Old Days of Credit Reporting

In the early days, when people bought things on credit at the general store, the clerk recorded their debts on a piece of paper that was then put into a paper tube, known as a "cuff," which they wore on their wrist.

Years later, someone had the idea of collecting the information from these cuffs and consolidating it so that merchants could review customers' credit histories before granting them credit. This system was seriously flawed, as it collected only bad information, failed to verify it, and never let the customers see it. The only groups that could access the data were lenders and merchants.

Thankfully, in the 1830s, the first third-party credit reporting agencies were set up as a network of offices across the nation, and they eventually turned into the CRAs we know today.

Ordering Your Credit Report

The law requires each of the major nationwide CRAs to give you a free copy of your credit report, at your request, once every 12 months.

So what are you waiting for? To order copies of your three credit reports online, visit www.annualcreditreport.com. To order by phone, call 877-322-8228. To order by mail, print out the request form from www.annualcreditreport.com, fill it out, and send it to: Annual Credit Report Request Service, P.O. Box 105281, Atlanta, GA 30348-5281. You'll get all three credit reports within a few weeks.

If you want to be really vigilant and order copies of your credit reports more than once a year, you can do so from the same website, by paying a fee. Or, you can start staggering your requests between the three CRAs, ordering one report approximately every four months from a different CRA. As long as you request only one report per CRA per year, it's still free.

Beware of Imposter CRAs

The Internet is littered with promotions for "free" credit reports, and many are backdoor efforts to sell credit-monitoring services and other products, according to the Federal Trade Commission.

These sites use misspellings and sound-alike names to misdirect consumers to sites unrelated to the government-mandated site. The FTC has sent letters to 130 impostor sites warning them that attempts to mislead consumers are illegal.

Researchers for the World Privacy Forum, a consumer education organization, found 112 sites that were using some combination or close spelling of "annual credit report."

Some of the sites asked for Social Security numbers, birth dates, and other sensitive information, the World Privacy Forum report said. Others directed consumers to sites that sell identity theft or other credit-related products and services, the report said.

Consumers land on impostor sites in two primary ways: by mistyping the name of the official Internet site, or by using a search engine and clicking on the wrong result, the report said.

If you're planning to exercise your right to order free credit reports, there are several ways to protect yourself:

- Link to the legitimate site through the Federal Trade Commission's Internet site, www.ftc.gov. When you go to www.ftc.gov, you'll see two buttons that link to the official site, says Lydia Parnes, director of the FTC's Bureau of Consumer Protection.

- Be wary of any site that promises a free credit report, then asks for your credit card number. That may be an indication that you've landed on an impostor site.

- Don't respond or reply to emails, pop-up ads, or phone calls that claim to come from www.annualcreditreport.com or one of the credit-reporting agencies. These may be scams seeking personal information.

 "Beware impostor offers of free credit report," by Sandra Block, August 22, 2005.

Reading Your Credit Report

Once you've received copies of your credit reports, you'll be able to see what the CRAs say about you. There's just one problem—credit reports can be confusing. If you feel a little overwhelmed when you see yours, you're certainly not alone. Use this step-by-step explanation to help you read and interpret each section.

What you'll find in your report

Your credit report is divided into four sections: identifying information, credit history, inquiries, and public records.

Identifying information. Your report will start with basic personal information: your name, current and recent addresses, the last four digits of your Social Security number, your date of birth, and current and previous employers.

Don't skip over these. Read every entry to make sure it's correct. One bad piece of information could be a sign of identity theft. For example, if your report lists current or previous addresses that you've never heard of, that could mean your file has been mixed with someone else's or that someone is using your identity.

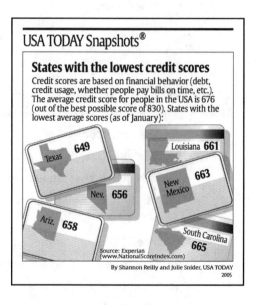

USA TODAY Snapshots®

States with the lowest credit scores

Credit scores are based on financial behavior (debt, credit usage, whether people pay bills on time, etc.). The average credit score for people in the USA is 676 (out of the best possible score of 830). States with the lowest average scores (as of January):

Texas **649**
Louisiana **661**
New Mexico **663**
Nev. **656**
Ariz. **658**
South Carolina **665**

Source: Experian (www.NationalScoreIndex.com)

By Shannon Reilly and Julie Snider, USA TODAY
2005

Credit history. Next, you'll see information specific to your credit history, such as details of every credit account you've ever opened, including the date opened, the credit limit or amount of the loan, the payment terms, the balance, and a payment history. Closed or inactive accounts stay on your report for seven to 11 years from the date of their last activity.

Decoding Your Credit History

The credit history section of your report will most likely include the following terms:

- **Company name:** Who reported the information.
- **Account number:** Don't expect to see your exact account number; this section may be encrypted for your protection.
- **Whose account:** What person is responsible for the account and what type of account it is. Here are the most common abbreviations:
  - **I** – Individual
  - **J** – Joint
  - **A** – Authorized User
  - **T** – Terminated.
- **Date opened:** Month and year.
- **Months reported:** How many months the account history has been reported for.
- **Last activity:** Date of the last activity on the account.
- **High credit:** Highest amount you've charged or your credit limit.
- **Terms:** Number of installments or the amount of the monthly payments.
- **Balance:** How much money you owe on the account.
- **Past due:** Overdue loan amounts.
- **Status:** Type of account and the timeliness of payment. Here are the most common abbreviations:
  - **O** – Open
  - **R** – Revolving
  - **I** – Installment.
- **Date reported:** The last time information on this account was reported by your creditor.

If you don't recognize a recently opened account, it may mean that a criminal has taken out a line of credit using your identity. Make sure it's not just an old, closed account that you've since forgotten. (We'll explain what to about such issues later in this chapter.)

If you or your creditors have ever disputed something on the report, this too will show up in this section.

Inquiries. Credit reporting agencies record an inquiry whenever a copy of your credit report is given to another party, such as a lender, service provider, landlord, or insurer. Inquiries stay on your credit report for up to two years.

TIP

Watch who's watching you. When reviewing the inquiries section of your credit report, watch closely for names of people or businesses that sound unfamiliar. If you find any, make it your business to find out who they are and why they're looking at your credit. If you don't recognize the supposed creditor accessing your report, it may be a sign of identity theft.

Public records. In some states, your credit report may contain information from government agencies, such as social services or police departments. Ever been evicted? Filed for bankruptcy? Failed to pay child support? These embarrassing details may show up on your credit report and stay there for seven years. But it could be that someone used your identity to do any of these things.

Who can request a copy of your report

With all the personal information your credit reports contain, you might think they'd be kept reasonably private. You'd be only partially right. The Fair Credit Reporting Act (FCRA) basically allows anyone with a "permissible purpose" to access your credit report. These people might include:

- potential lenders
- landlords

- insurance companies
- employers and potential employers
- identity theft protection companies
- a state or local child support enforcement agency
- any government agency
- service providers (i.e., cell phone or cable companies), and
- an individual or company that has your written authorization to obtain your credit report.

Naturally, this list doesn't include identity thieves. Nevertheless, they find ways to access your report, for example by posing as a business or landlord. That gives the thief instant access to information on where you work and live, the credit accounts that have been opened in your name, how you pay your bills, and more—everything they need to assume your identity. In most cases, they don't even need your permission. (Only current or future employers must get your written consent to request a report; as well as anyone requesting your medical information.)

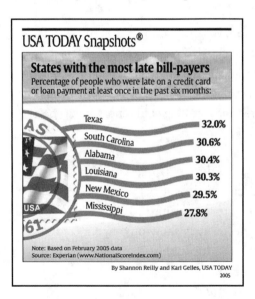

USA TODAY Snapshots®

States with the most late bill-payers
Percentage of people who were late on a credit card or loan payment at least once in the past six months:

Texas	32.0%
South Carolina	30.6%
Alabama	30.4%
Louisiana	30.3%
New Mexico	29.5%
Mississippi	27.8%

Note: Based on February 2005 data
Source: Experian (www.NationalScoreIndex.com)

By Shannon Reilly and Karl Gelles, USA TODAY 2005

A related problem is that companies can buy your name and address from a CRA in order to mail or call you for marketing purposes or with offers of preapproved credit cards. While these companies aren't allowed to see your actual credit report, they'll ask the CRA for a list of people who match certain criteria—for example, those whose FICO scores are in a certain range. CRAs make money selling your information to others and have been known to deliver this information into the hands of criminals.

If you don't want to have your name sold to these companies, you can opt out by either writing to the three CRAs or by calling 888-5-OPTOUT (888-567-8688). This will remove your name for two years from mailing and telemarketing lists that come from the three CRAs.

The fact that so many people can view such an extensive snapshot of your life may be nerve-wracking. If it's any comfort, CRAs do play an important role. If borrowers, especially those with poor credit, were able to hide their credit history information, lenders would most likely respond by limiting access to credit, especially at reasonable interest rates. In countries without credit reporting, lenders are forced to use more intrusive methods to assess credit risk, such as visiting an applicant's home or business, getting character references, and insisting on cosigners on loans.

What's Not in Your Report

You won't find information on any of the following in your credit report:
- Your checking or savings accounts
- Bankruptcies that are more than ten years old
- Debts that have been charged off (deemed uncollectible) or placed for collection, if they're more than seven years old
- Gender
- Ethnicity
- Religion
- Political affiliation
- Medical history
- Criminal records.

Correcting Errors on Your Credit Report

Imagine this scenario: You've just been turned down for an auto loan because your credit report shows you missed several payments on your credit card. But wait—you don't recognize the name of the bank and you've never made a late payment on anything.

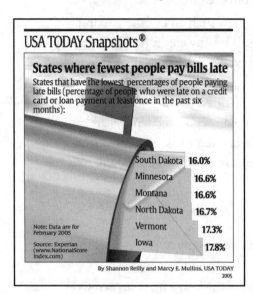

USA TODAY Snapshots®

States where fewest people pay bills late

States that have the lowest percentages of people paying late bills (percentage of people who were late on a credit card or loan payment at least once in the past six months):

South Dakota	16.0%
Minnesota	16.6%
Montana	16.6%
North Dakota	16.7%
Vermont	17.3%
Iowa	17.8%

Note: Data are for February 2005

Source: Experian (www.NationalScore Index.com)

By Shannon Reilly and Marcy E. Mullins, USA TODAY 2005

Sound unlikely? It's not. According to the U.S. Public Interest Research Group, three-quarters of all credit reports contain errors, many of which are serious enough to prevent you from being approved for a loan. And a number of these errors are caused by identity theft. We'll talk in later chapters about how to deal with all the financial and other effects of identity theft. But let's focus here on how to get your credit report cleaned up.

File a dispute

If you find your credit report marred by erroneous information or identity theft, federal law gives you the right to ask that these mistakes be corrected. You can dispute it with whichever CRA shows the error. Contact the agency according to its rules, which can be found on its website. All three agencies (Experian, Equifax, and TransUnion) allow consumers to submit disputes online, on the phone, or via snail mail.

If you use snail mail, send a certified letter that clearly states the facts and explains why you're disputing the item. Include a copy of your report with the mistake highlighted. Include copies (not originals) of any documents that support your position, such as a copy of the police report you've filed regarding the identity theft (described below). Also

Case of the Wrong David

After graduating from high school, David Joe Hernandez served four years in the Air Force at bases in New Mexico and Japan. So it came as a shock when he returned home to Oak Forest, Illinois, and discovered collections agents were hunting him down to make good on some 20 delinquent accounts.

Hernandez spent hours trying to clear up the mistakes through Experian, Equifax, and TransUnion, the Big Three credit-reporting agencies. But things got worse. He learned he was linked to a string of felonies, including a drug charge that hindered him from landing a job at Best Buy. Then in August 2006, state regulators began garnishing his wages to pay child support to a woman in Chicago he'd never heard of.

While he lived a low-key military life, Hernandez's identity was hit by a double whammy. A crook in Chicago used his Social Security number to create and siphon new accounts.

Hernandez first became aware of the problems after he was discharged from the military and returned from a 16-month tour of duty at Misawa Air Base in Japan. First National Bank of Chicago called him seeking payment of a delinquent $4,500 loan.

He ultimately learned that the Big Three credit bureaus listed him as responsible for 20 delinquent accounts for cell phone bills, credit cards, utility bills, and hospital bills. "All of the billing addresses were to places in Chicago—places I'd never lived," he says.

Hernandez spent much of his free time for the next year and a half on the phone or corresponding with the credit bureaus and creditors.

Hernandez believes the continued attempts to use his name have hurt his credit rating. "I've done everything I could to keep up good credit, but no matter what I do, I come up losing," he says.

 "While he served abroad, his credit was under siege," by Byron Acohido and Jon Swartz, June 5, 2007.

pay a little extra to include a "return receipt" request with your letter, so that the postal service will send you a postcard confirming that the CRA received it.

The credit-reporting agencies are legally obligated to respond to your dispute by initiating an investigation and, if appropriate, collecting evidence from your creditors. If they find that the reported information is indeed inaccurate, they must either remove or correct it, usually within 30 days.

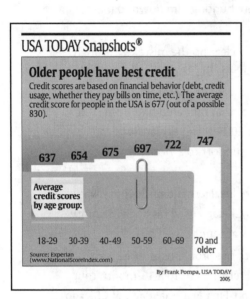

USA TODAY Snapshots®

Older people have best credit

Credit scores are based on financial behavior (debt, credit usage, whether they pay bills on time, etc.). The average credit score for people in the USA is 677 (out of a possible 830).

Average credit scores by age group:

18-29	30-39	40-49	50-59	60-69	70 and older
637	654	675	697	722	747

Source: Experian (www.NationalScoreIndex.com)

By Frank Pompa, USA TODAY 2005

Deal with denials

After investigating, the CRAs may refuse to remove the disputed information under certain narrow circumstances (like if they suspect you're lying about the identity theft, which some people do to stall their creditors). However, they'll need to notify you in writing of this decision.

At that point, you should send a letter of dispute to the creditor whose reporting statements you believe to be incorrect. You'll find the creditor's contact information within the CRA's notice to you. Keep copies of all correspondence, and keep notes of your conversations (with the date) if you call a CRA on the phone.

If you're unable to resolve a dispute, you have the right to add a 100-word comment to your credit report. This alerts creditors that there is an unresolved issue in your report.

Block fraudulent information

If the error in your report isn't a garden-variety mistake, but appears to be an instance of identity theft, you've got another remedy at your disposal—and one that you should act on right away. Ask to block the reporting of any information in your report that is the result of identity theft. This may cover accounts that were opened or soiled by the thief, inquiries that were initiated by the thief, and other erroneous negative information. Once the CRA gets the necessary information from you, it has four days in which to place the block.

Before doing this, you must first file an Identity Theft Complaint Form with your local police, in which you provide details about your identity theft case, such as which accounts were opened or misused by scammers. It's used to give CRAs and creditors the information they need to verify that you're a victim—and to show which accounts and inaccurate information are the result of identity theft. The CRA may deny your request for a block if you don't supply this report or if you misrepresent facts. Find the necessary form at www.ftc.gov (under "Quick Finder," click "Identity Theft," then, next to "If your information has been stolen and used by an identity thief," click "more," then follow the links under "File a report with your local police ...").

Place a fraud alert on your file

If the error in your file was due to identity theft, you should also ask that a fraud alert be placed on your file. The alert tells potential creditors to verify your identity before issuing new credit in your name, although they're still able to access your credit report. Anyone can ask for a 90-day fraud alert, while only victims of identity theft can ask for or an extended fraud alert (seven years, with evidence that you've been victimized, such as a police report or Identity Theft Complaint).

While a great step toward protecting your identity, fraud alerts aren't foolproof. Because of successful lobbying efforts by the financial services industry, creditors are permitted leeway in how they verify your identity, The law requires only that creditors take "reasonable steps" by way of verification, and doesn't fully define what these steps should be. Cases exist in which fraud alerts were actually ignored by lax lenders. In such a scenario, a thief could get credit in your name despite the presence of a fraud alert.

Sample Letter to Credit-Reporting Agencies

[*Your name*]

[*Street address*]

[*City, state, ZIP code*]

[*Your phone number*]

[*Your email address*]

[Date]

Subject: Identity Theft

[*Name of credit-reporting agency*]

[*Street address*]

[*City, state, ZIP code*]

To Whom It May Concern:

I am a victim of identity theft. I am writing to request that you block the following fraudulent information from my credit report: [*describe item(s) to be blocked, including name of source, such as creditors or tax court, and type of item, such as credit account or judgment.*]

This information does not relate to any transaction that I have made. I have enclosed a copy of my Identity Theft Report. In accordance with section 605B of the Fair Credit Reporting Act, please block this fraudulent information on my credit report, which is the result of identity theft. Please let me know if you need any other information from me.

Sincerely,

[*Sign your name*]

[*Print your name*]

Enclosures:

Proof of identification [*preferably a copy of your driver's license*]

Utility bill (to verify address)

Completed Identity Theft Complaint or police report [*if available*]

Letting a Credit-Monitoring Service Check on Your Report

While getting the occasional free credit report is a good, if rudimentary way to spot identity theft, it leaves you essentially unprotected in the weeks or months between requesting your reports. To find out about identity theft more quickly—and with less work—you might consider subscribing to a credit-monitoring service.

A credit-monitoring service will alert you to certain high-risk changes that occur in your credit report. For example, if a thief opens new accounts in your name, you'll usually find out within a day or so. What credit monitoring won't do is stop the theft in the first place. And you'll still have a role to play: If you receive an alert about a suspicious inquiry, you'll have to contact the CRAs as well as your bank or credit card company to let them know.

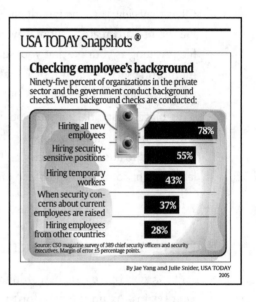

USA TODAY Snapshots ®

Checking employee's background

Ninety-five percent of organizations in the private sector and the government conduct background checks. When background checks are conducted:

Hiring all new employees — 78%
Hiring security-sensitive positions — 55%
Hiring temporary workers — 43%
When security concerns about current employees are raised — 37%
Hiring employees from other countries — 28%

Source: CSO magazine survey of 389 chief security officers and security executives. Margin of error ±5 percentage points.

By Jae Yang and Julie Snider, USA TODAY
2005

If you're considering signing up, make sure you understand what you're getting before you buy. Prices and services among credit-monitoring services vary widely. Some monitor only one of the three major CRAs. Stick to services sold by Equifax, Experian, or TransUnion for the best quality at a reasonable price.

TIP
Credit-monitoring agencies may not flag every fraudulent use of your Social Security number. In a scam called "synthetic identity theft," thieves combine a real number with a fictitious name and other information to create a whole new (but fake) person. They then establish new accounts with their fictional identities.

If enough new data comes in with your Social Security number, the CRAs may view the new identity as legitimate and create a separate file (or instead create a "subfile," which remains associated with your file). As long as your file and your identity thief's file are separate, a monitoring service will not pick that up. You may not even be allowed to see the file that has your SSN but not your name.

The biggest potential harm to you may be if your Social Security number ends up in databases recording the thief's criminal activity—and you're then asked to answer for the crimes. In addition, a hypervigilant debt collector might come after you based on the Social Security number alone.

Putting a Freeze on Future Identity Theft

A credit freeze is one of the best things you can do to stop identity theft before it begins. Assuming you don't plan to take out a lot of loans in the near future, the freeze will hardly interfere with your everyday life at all.

What a credit freeze does

A credit freeze prevents potential new creditors from viewing your credit report without your permission. So when an identity thief tries to take out a car loan or get a credit card in your name, you'll be the first to know. It's excellent protection against the vast majority of identity theft, in which criminals open new accounts using your identity or pieces of your identity. In cases where they arrange for the bills to go to their own address, you'd have no immediate way of knowing you've been victimized.

Placing a credit freeze does not affect your credit score, nor does it stop you from getting your free annual credit report, nor from buying your credit score. However, if you want to apply for a loan or line of credit, or allow someone new (with whom you're not already doing business) to access your credit report, you must temporarily lift the freeze (as described below).

Clearly, credit freezes aren't for everyone. If you're the kind of person who frequently applies for credit on short notice, you may want to steer clear of them. If, however, you've already been the victim of identity theft, rarely use credit, or are just generally protective of your identity, a credit freeze provides exceptional protection and peace of mind.

Freezing Out ID Theft

Like many victims of identity theft, Steven Comeau learned of the crime when a collection agency called and asked why he wasn't paying his bills. But Comeau's case was anything but typical. Criminals had used his personal information to get a mortgage on a rental property in Brooklyn, New York.

That was in 2001, and Comeau, an information technology manager in South Brunswick, New Jersey, was in 2005 still trying to convince people he's not a deadbeat landlord. In addition to calls from collection agents, he's gotten complaints from tenants. When Comeau and his wife, Magda, put an offer on a house in November, they discovered that his credit report listed a mortgage default. In April, he received a call from a lawyer for an investment bank that wanted to buy the building. "It never ends," he says.

Comeau believes the fallout from the scam would have been significantly reduced if he had frozen his credit reports.

 "Is freezing your credit the way to safeguard your ID?" by Sandra Block, June 19, 2005.

What a credit freeze doesn't do

Now, the limitations: While a credit freeze can prevent an identity thief from opening new accounts in your name, it cannot protect your existing accounts from fraud. You'll still need to monitor your credit report and financial account statements regularly to look for potential fraud on existing accounts.

In addition, if a thief has already started the identity theft process at the time you place the credit freeze, the freeze itself probably won't be able to stop it, as the thief may have already used your identity to apply for credit.

Is Your Bank's Identity Protection Enough?

Many people mistakenly believe they are protected by the banks or other financial institutions that issue their credit and debit cards.

It's true that banks and credit card companies typically monitor your accounts for fraud. Credit card companies, for example, look for suspicious patterns of charges, and often freeze account access until you confirm the charges are yours. But they can't catch everything—and many thieves start with small charges, to create a pattern of behavior that neither you nor the bank or credit card company notice until it's too late.

Also, this type of protection doesn't cover cases where a fraudster sets up a new account in your name. The thief will make sure that the bank sends all correspondence straight to the thief—most likely leaving you oblivious to the damage being done.

How to freeze your credit

All three CRAs allow consumers in all states to freeze their credit reports, whether they're identity theft victims or not. To place a credit freeze, send a request letter to each of the three CRAs. (Unlike a fraud alert, making the request of one agency is not enough.) The letter should include your name, address, and the last four digits of your Social Security number. If you have filed a police report or Identity Theft Complaint, include it, as well. Here are the mailing addresses:

Equifax Security Freeze
P.O. Box 105788
Atlanta, GA 30348

Experian Security Freeze
P.O. Box 9554
Allen, TX 75013

TransUnion Security Freeze
P.O. Box 6790
Fullerton, CA 92834-6790

The cost of placing a credit freeze (and also of temporarily lifting and removing it) varies from state to state. (For details, go to www.stoppingidtheft.org.) Many states' laws mandate that credit freezes be free for identity theft victims who can provide a police report or Identity Theft Complaint, while in other states, the CRAs are allowed to charge all consumers a fee—typically $10. (And you'll have to pay the fee three times, in order to place the freeze with all three CRAs.) Some states also waive the fees for senior citizens.

The CRAs must freeze your files within five business days of receiving your written request; or, if you're a victim of identity theft, within 24 hours of getting the police report and information confirming

USA TODAY Snapshots®

Postal offenses
Number of arrests in top postal crimes in 2005:

6,788
Mail theft 1,855
Mailing of controlled substances 1,577
Mail fraud

Source: U.S. Postal Inspection Service
By David Stuckey and Frank Pompa, USA TODAY 2007

your identity. The CRAs will send you written notice that the freeze is in place within five days of it going into effect. This confirmation will include:

- a Personal Identification Number (PIN); and
- instructions on how to lift or remove the freeze.

Additionally, if you subscribe to a credit-monitoring service directly from one of the CRAs, you may be able to freeze your credit reports as part of the service. But this protection will extend only to the CRA from which you bought the service, not to the other two.

How to lift the freeze

What happens when you want to apply for a mortgage, other loan, or credit card? You'll need to contact all three CRAs and ask to unfreeze your credit reports. In most states, they'll be legally allowed three business days within which to temporarily lift or remove your freeze. That can be a major hurdle if you're trying to get a loan on short notice.

But, as USA TODAY's Sandra Block explains, "Under laws that took effect September 1, 2008, residents of Arizona, Idaho, New Mexico, Utah, Wyoming, and Washington, DC, can lift or remove a credit freeze in 15 minutes, using a personal identification number, according to Consumers Union. And starting in January 2009, the 15-minute provision will extend to Indiana, Maryland, Montana, Nebraska, and Tennessee."

Block adds, "You might also have to pay a fee to suspend or end the freeze."

Keep Prying Eyes Off Your Financial Accounts

When standing in line at your local department store, buying that perfect birthday gift for Mom, you need to decide how to pay for it. Will you use cash? A check? Or some form of plastic, either a credit card or a debit card (which automatically deducts the money from your bank account)?

If you're like most people, you use a combination of paper, plastic, and electronic payment methods in your daily life—and not just when you're out shopping. To save time and money on your monthly bills, you may switch your various billing accounts to autopilot, authorizing an automatic deduction from your bank account. These choices undoubtedly make life easier for you, but they also may be pushing you one step closer to becoming an identity theft victim.

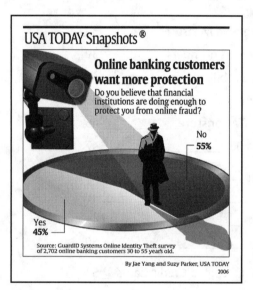

USA TODAY Snapshots®

Online banking customers want more protection

Do you believe that financial institutions are doing enough to protect you from online fraud?

No 55%

Yes 45%

Source: GuardID Systems Online Identity Theft survey of 2,702 online banking customers 30 to 55 years old.

By Jae Yang and Suzy Parker, USA TODAY 2006

Unfortunately, there's no risk-free method of paying for things. Every time you hand over your credit card to a waitress, you may be giving an identity thief the opportunity to steal your account details. When you write a check at the doctor's office, someone might copy your personal information. When you take out money at the ATM, someone might watch you type in your PIN and use it to steal your money. And while carrying cash in your purse or wallet may help avoid identity thieves, you could end up losing it to regular old thieves, or simply drop your wallet. (That's part of why credit cards became popular in the first place.)

But these aren't reasons to live in fear. Simply understanding the types of risk associated with each type of payment will go a long way toward minimizing your financial exposure. In this chapter, you'll learn about the sensitivity factor (amount of risk and protection) associated with each major type of payment—credit cards, debit cards, and checks. You'll also learn prevention tactics to guard against identity theft, how to use the laws that govern identity theft and other security violations, and the first steps to take to report and deal with a theft.

Paying With Plastic: Risks and Protective Measures

"The future, my boy, is in plastics," said Dustin Hoffman's neighbor in the 1967 hit movie, *The Graduate*. While he wasn't talking about credit cards, his statement sounds especially prescient today. Most U.S. adults own at least one credit card and one debit card. Credit cards are the most popular method of spending money (including for Internet purchases).

If you're like most people, you pull out your credit or ATM/debit card without thinking much about the potential consequences. But let's look closer at what could happen, and how to stop it.

Bold-faced theft of your card or card numbers

One of the biggest problems with both credit and debit cards is that they can literally fall into the wrong hands, whether by loss or theft. For example, in May 2008, USA TODAY reported that a couple of young jetsetters financed their luxury lifestyle using credit card and bank account information

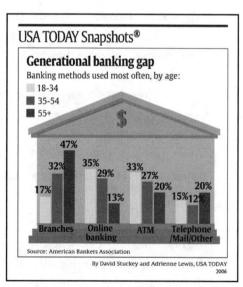

USA TODAY Snapshots®

Generational banking gap
Banking methods used most often, by age:
- 18-34
- 35-54
- 55+

Branches: 32%, 17%, 47%
Online banking: 35%, 29%, 13%
ATM: 33%, 27%, 20%
Telephone/Mail/Other: 20%, 15%, 12%

Source: American Bankers Association

By David Stuckey and Adrienne Lewis, USA TODAY 2006

they'd stolen from friends, coworkers, and neighbors. Jocelyn Kirsch and Edward K. Anderton allegedly used the stolen data to finance lavish purchases and travel, including a trip to Paris. They were arrested when they went to pick up a package, containing expensive lingerie, at a local UPS store using a neighbor's identification.

If You Can't Trust Your Pizza Waiter...

Not all identity thieves are lurking in the shadows. Many, including the two described below, are waiters and other workers who process people's credit cards, and decide to, shall we say, augment their tips. Since there's little you can do to prevent this, take these tales as a reason to keep tabs on your credit card statements and history (discussed later in this chapter).

In January 2008, a (by-then former) Pizza Hut employee reportedly used customer credit card and debit card accounts to rack up $6,700 in Internet charges. She'd simply copied bank card numbers and customer names, taken them home, and gone shopping online.

Just a month earlier, a Wendy's fast food employee made the news when she was charged with stealing credit card numbers from customers of the drive-through booth where she worked. Right after running people's cards through the store device, she'd swipe them through her own personal credit-card reading device, which was small enough to keep in her pocket. (Police said these devices are readily available on the Internet for less than $100.) Once she'd run the cards, she'd allegedly hook her reader up to her laptop to access the numbers and use them for—you guessed it—online shopping.

This isn't the only case where friends and neighbors have turned out to be the perpetrators of identity crimes. While pickpockets, muggers, scammers, and other criminals account for a good half of identity theft, guess who experts say makes up the other half? Family members, friends, coworkers, or other people known to the victim. That means it can be as important to protect the information in your files at home and at work as what's in your wallet.

Here are some general tips for preventing or finding out about theft of your credit or debit card or your card numbers. We'll give more specific tips related to particular schemes and scams in the coming sections.

- **Monitor your credit card, bank statements, and telephone bills.** This is critical—reading your statements is sometimes the only way to find out that your identity has been stolen. Place a mark on each month of your calendar showing when your statements should arrive, and follow up if you don't get them. Reconcile your monthly statements with your receipts, and report any discrepancies as soon as you find them.

  Going for the gold.
  Identity thieves particularly like to get access to gold and platinum credit cards, with their high credit limits. The high limits not only allow for some luxury shopping, but mean the credit card company is less likely to notice unusual activity on the account.

- **Don't put outgoing credit card or other bill payments in an accessible mailbox.** An identity thief who sees the envelope sticking out of your mailbox can retrieve it in seconds, and you'll assume your mail delivery person took it. It's safest to mail bills inside a post office (even corner mailboxes have, on rare occasions, been robbed).

- **Shred your receipts and old credit card or bank records.** When you get a receipt from a credit or debit card transaction, take it home and shred it instead of throwing it in the trash. Never leave receipts lying around. Also shred credit card and bank records when they're no longer needed—after seven years is usually long enough (though you should never throw out records proving an identity theft). And if you close a card account, snip up the card before tossing it.

- **Carry only as many credit cards as you regularly need.** For example, the card for a department store you visit only at its semiannual sale can stay at home until the next visit.

- **Keep financial records in a secure place within your house.** A locked filing cabinet is best.

- **After a home burglary, think identity theft.** Your jewelry and laptop may not be the only thing stolen—the burglars may well have taken documents with your personal or financial information. Because it's hard to tell for sure, assume you're a victim and take the follow-up steps described in Chapter 11.

In addition to the risks you face when carrying or using your credit and debit cards, there are risks during the card-approval process that are completely out of your control. In 2007, for example, USA TODAY reported that more than four million customer accounts at grocery stores in the Northeast and Florida were exposed to fraud when hackers intercepted wireless transfers of customer information. (And this was despite the fact that Hannaford Bros. Co., which owns the grocery stores, met the latest standards for data security.) About 4.2 million credit and debit card numbers were exposed and at least 1,800 stolen during the seconds it takes for that information to travel from the card-swiping customer to the credit card companies for approval. We'll dive deeper into data breaches and what you can do about them in Chapter 7.

Cramming extra charges onto your bills

A scam called "cramming" involves unethical or even fictional companies adding charges to your phone or credit card bills for services you never received. While they sometimes get ahold of your information in indirect ways, such as through dumpster diving or the black market, more often you've handed over your card number or telephone number voluntarily. That is, you've signed up for or ordered something—perhaps a travel subscription, trial offer, or online adult entertainment service—from a seemingly legit company, without having read the fine print. If you're billed for something that was never authorized by you or someone you know, such as Internet access or phone sex charges, it's likely that you've been crammed.

Typically, the credit card or telephone company that processes these charges simply passes them on to consumers. After all, they have no way of knowing whether the charges are correct or incorrect. It's up to you to monitor your bills and dispute inappropriate charges.

When you complain to your bank or telephone company, it in turn will contact the company that reported the charges, which will most likely respond by politely canceling the charges—they know there are plenty more people out there who won't even notice. That's assuming the company is still around—many have disappeared by the time the disputes start rolling in. If that happens with a phone charge, you can ask the telephone company to reverse the charges, but you may face an uphill battle proving the fraud actually happened.

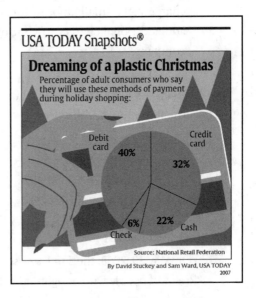

USA TODAY Snapshots®

Dreaming of a plastic Christmas
Percentage of adult consumers who say they will use these methods of payment during holiday shopping:

Debit card 40%
Credit card 32%
Cash 22%
Check 6%

Source: National Retail Federation

By David Stuckey and Sam Ward, USA TODAY
2007

Consider this scenario. Alan is a single man looking for love. One night, he comes across a newspaper advertisement for a "free matching" service that connects singles. He calls the toll-free number, and a representative asks him for his phone number and promises to connect him with a local single. Soon, he receives numerous return calls, which turn out to be from the service's employees posing as "local singles." They do not disclose that they're charging him for the calls, even though the ad said that the service was "free."

Alan might notice that his next phone bill includes several charges, stated as collect or direct calls from an unfamiliar number...or he might just hurriedly pay the bill. Some people have been billed hundreds of dollars on their phone bills for services delivered through return calls.

To avoid cramming scams:

- **Carefully check your bills and financial statements each month.** If you see any charges that look suspicious, notify the sender immediately.

- **Make noise.** If you're charged for something you didn't order, or for a subscription you've tried to cancel, dispute the charge, preferably both by phone and in writing.

- **Don't give your credit card or phone number to an adult site.** They're notorious for conducting cramming scams, in which they charge you a small amount for some type of service and then add additional charges to your bill, often disguised as another company.

- **Read the fine print before signing up for any subscription or service.** Often, the fine print includes verbiage that puts you on the hook for monthly fees.

Scammers Use Gas Station Skimmers

Here's something to think about next time you're swiping your debit card to purchase gas.

On May 30, 2008, the *San Francisco Chronicle* reported that dozens of people who bought gas with their debit cards at an Arco station in San Jose had a total of $45,000 drained from their bank accounts by identity thieves who used skimming techniques.

The con artists attached a card-reading device, or skimmer, to a payment terminal at the gas station. The device collected victims' debit card information, including PINs. The thieves then transferred the information to blank magnetic-stripped cards, which they used to withdraw cash at ATMs across California.

Police believe that the same thieves also targeted Arco stations statewide, probably because Arco stations accept only debit cards—no credit cards allowed. This gives thieves more opportunities to steal bank card numbers and PINs.

Shaving, cutting, and pasting numbers onto a new card

In a scam called "shaving," thieves don't even need to steal your actual credit card or your personal information to start using your credit card account. All they need is your credit card number, which some of them actually guess, by simply trying out different combinations of 16-digit number sequences on an online shopping site or a credit card machine. Eventually, they find a number that works. Then, they physically shave numbers off gift cards or old credit cards and glue them onto another credit card. They use this homemade credit card for online and offline purchases. Your credit card never leaves your wallet.

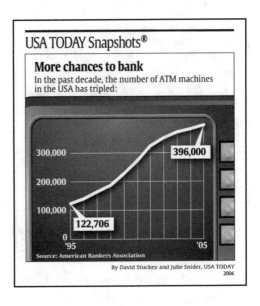

USA TODAY Snapshots®

More chances to bank
In the past decade, the number of ATM machines in the USA has tripled:

396,000

300,000

200,000

100,000

122,706

0

'95   '05

Source: American Bankers Association

By David Stuckey and Julie Snider, USA TODAY
2006

Shaving is all but impossible to prevent, so early detection is your best bet. Be sure to:

- **Monitor your credit card billing statements closely.** Even a small charge may indicate a test run by the thief, who will move on to bigger purchases soon.
- **Notify your creditor as quickly as possible after you learn of any fraudulent transactions.** This will help prevent future charges.

Skimming your number at the ATM or store

In a particularly frustrating type of scam, you might use your card for a legitimate transaction—such as to withdraw money from your ATM or settle the bill at a restaurant—only to have an identity thief access your card number using a device called a "skimmer." Most skimmers are installed on ATM machines, and are hard to detect. A small device fits over the normal card reading slot, reading your card's magnetic stripe when you swipe your card. Other skimmers are handheld devices that dishonest merchants, wait staff, or store employees keep in their pockets and run your card through during the few minutes that it's in their possession.

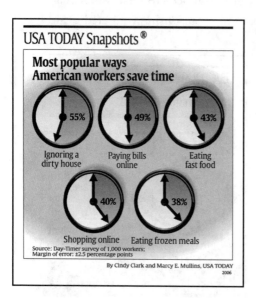

USA TODAY Snapshots®

Most popular ways American workers save time

- 55% Ignoring a dirty house
- 49% Paying bills online
- 43% Eating fast food
- 40% Shopping online
- 38% Eating frozen meals

Source: Day-Timer survey of 1,000 workers; Margin of error: ±2.5 percentage points

By Cindy Clark and Marcy E. Mullins, USA TODAY
2006

In 2007, the *Today* show team, in partnership with Washington Mutual Bank, set up an unauthorized card reader (purchased online) at the door of one of their New York City branches. The branch did not require customers to scan their cards to get in, so their theory was that people would scan their cards through this fake machine anyway. They were right—16 people opened the door without swiping the card, but 18 people swiped their card through the unauthorized reader. If these people's cards had had the Visa or MasterCard logo on them, they could have immediately been used for online transactions, even without their PIN code.

Use these techniques to avoid getting caught in a skimming scam:

- **Use secure ATM machines under video surveillance or inside of a bank.** Thieves face greater risk installing skimmers where there are security cameras or other forms of protection. The security cameras are usually embedded within the machine itself—be wary of any camera that looks like it could have been installed by a passerby. Also avoid ATMs that aren't affiliated with a bank.

- **Be alert.** Skimming devices usually stick out a few extra inches from an ATM or payment machine. If you notice something strange, find another machine.

- **Don't fall for temporary fixes.** Never use a machine that has a sticker or sign that says "Swipe Here," or "Machine Broken—

Swipe Here." A legitimate machine will not instruct you to do anything out of the ordinary.

- **When in doubt, don't let merchants handle your cards without your presence.** The tradition of letting your waitress walk off with your card is fine in places you trust, but at least consider taking your card straight up to the counter when you're on unfamiliar ground.

- **Act quickly if there's a problem.** If a machine keeps your card, call your bank immediately.

Shoulder surfing (watch your back!)

"Shoulder surfing" is another popular technique used by identity thieves, especially in crowded places such as cafés or restaurants. For instance, as you enter your PIN at a gas station, an identity thief may stand behind you, memorize your information, and later steal your card. This is why you should always be alert when using your card in a public place. Also keep in mind that anyone could be an identity thief, including the coffee shop employee idly watching you enter your PIN in the card reader.

In many cases, recording or memorizing your PIN number is the thief's prelude to stealing your card. If a thief gets ahold of your PIN, it increases your risk of physical danger in the form of a mugging or break-in later.

Use the tips provided below to prevent or detect shoulder surfers and others who might steal your PIN.

- **Memorize your PIN.** Don't carry it in your purse or wallet or write it on your card. Also, avoid writing your PIN on a deposit slip or deposit envelope.

- **Avoid prying eyes.** When you're at the ATM, checkout counter, or anywhere else where you'll need to punch in your PIN, position your body so that no person or surveillance camera can see your fingers in action.

Magstripe Scams

When it comes to data storage, the familiar "magstripe" on the back of your plastic cards is about as simple and ubiquitous a piece of technology as you can find. Consisting of magnetized particles impregnated on a thin band, it is the decades-old technology that makes credit, debit, and gift card transactions possible. It is also widely used on employee access cards, public transit tokens, phone calling cards, even hotel card keys.

Now the lowly magstripe has become a favorite tool of identity thieves on the cutting edge, say law enforcement officials and tech security analysts.

The arrest of a suspected identity thief in Edmonton, Alberta, shed light on one recent inventive scam.

Acting on a tip, Edmonton police arrested a 26-year-old man sitting in a shopping mall restaurant typing away on his laptop, and in possession of thumb drives and computer printouts of credit card account data stolen from hundreds of U.S. and Canadian bank customers.

The suspect also had several prepaid gift cards issued by Visa and MasterCard, and a device for embedding data on a magstripe, called a "magstripe reader-writer," says the arresting officer, Edmonton Detective Bob Gauthier.

By altering the magstripes of authentic bank gift cards, the suspect bypassed a difficult and risky step other magstripe scammers are forced to take: fabricating fake credit cards.

"Instead of having to make fake plastic, you can load up bank gift cards with stolen data you get from people online, then go in and use them like cash," Gauthier says.

 "Beware impostor offers of free credit report," by Sandra Block, August 22, 2005.

Credit Cards of the Future

As the bad guys continue to use technology to come up with ever-more sophisticated ways to commit credit card fraud, the good guys are fighting back. Companies are now creating new credit card technology that may change the way credit cards are used...and misused.

One recent invention is a wafer-thin card with an electronic display that periodically changes several digits of the card number, preventing anyone who wants to capture or copy the number from reusing it. The card has the same size and shape as a usual one. The difference is that its software is based on time. The card knows what time it is and is synchronized with credit card servers. Unfortunately, this technology hasn't yet become available to consumers.

Your Financial Consequences After Credit or Debit Card Fraud

Legal and consumer protections are in place to help you, so long as you abide by their time limits and other terms. The literature given to you by your credit or debit card company will tell you what protections it provides, usually based on various requirements in the federal laws (the federal Fair Credit Billing Act (FCBA), and the Electronic Funds Transfer Act (EFTA)).

Credit card protections

Credit cards offer particularly strong consumer protection. If you report a loss or theft before your card is used, the laws prohibit your card issuer from holding you responsible for any of the resulting charges. If the thief has already made charges by the time you discover the problem, you'll be responsible for only $50 in charges if you make a report within 60 days.

Another important legal protection is that credit card consumers may refuse to pay bills for goods that they never receive, or that are defective or otherwise unacceptable. That means that, if your credit card is stolen or compromised, you'll have an opportunity to dispute the fraudulent transaction before you pay the bill—you won't have to pay until the investigation is concluded.

ATM or debit card protections

With ATM or debit cards, if you report the card missing before it's been used fraudulently, you can't be held responsible for any unauthorized purchases (just like with credit cards). If you make the report within two days of discovering the theft, you can be held responsible for up to $50 in losses. Wait up to 60 days, and your liability increases to $500. If you fail to report unauthorized transactions within 60 days after your bank mails you the statement that includes unauthorized transactions, you may lose all the money in your account and be responsible for paying off any additional charges—possibly even the fees for checks bounced as a result of the plundering of your account!

USA TODAY Snapshots®

Credit card vs. debit card

Which one is safer to use?

Don't mind
49% Credit card
32% Debit card
19%

Source: Mintel/Greenfield Online survey of 1,299 adults 18 and older. Margin of error ±2 percentage points.

By Jae Yang and Veronica Salazar, USA TODAY 2006

If the fraudulent use of your debit card involves only your card number and not your physical card, you're liable only for losses that occur after 60 days from the date your bank mails you the statement that includes the fraudulent transactions. Once you inform your bank of the fraud, you're not responsible for any ongoing unauthorized charges.

Before You're a Victim: Switch From Debit to Credit Cards

At many points before, during, and after you use your credit or debit card, your information can be stolen and misused. But while credit cards and debit cards may look the same—and both may even have a logo (usually Visa or MasterCard) on the front—they have a few important differences when it comes to identity theft. The bottom line: Debit cards are riskier, and you may want to consider switching to credit cards.

When you pay with a credit card, you're essentially taking out a loan. The merchant, via a card network, electronically contacts your card issuer to verify your account number, expiration date, and credit availability before authorizing your transaction. The card issuer pays the merchant, and you're billed in your next statement.

USA TODAY Snapshots®

Checking out

Top reasons why families don't have checking accounts:

Do not write enough checks	28%
Do not like dealing with banks	23%
Not enough money	14%
Service charges too high	12%
Cannot balance an account	7%

Source: The Federal Reserve Board's Survey of Consumer Finances, 2004

By David Stuckey and Suzy Parker, USA TODAY 2007

Debit cards, by contrast, work more like checks. The money is withdrawn directly from your bank account when you buy something, and the only limit is the amount in your account.

If one of your cards—be it credit or debit—is lost or stolen, the thief can freely use it right up until you notify the bank and cancel the card. (That's why most card issuers offer 24-hour toll-free telephone numbers for you to call.) That could leave the thief a lot of shopping time while you're still in the dark about the theft. The thief will be especially happy if you have a debit card connected to a bank account with a high balance. Although you may be able to recoup some of what the thief spends during that precancellation spree, the bank may (in some cases) immediately deduct money from your bank account when the card was fraudulently used, after which you'll have to fight to get it back. See Chapter 11 details on what to do after misuse of either your debit or credit card.

So if you're currently using your debit card to make most purchases, consider making the switch to credit cards. Or if you must stick with a debit card, read the fine print on your debit card agreement to see what protection is offered. More and more debit card companies are extending the same consumer protections that cover credit cards.

> **TIP**
> **Make photocopies of any cards you carry, front and back.** Store the copies in a locked place at home. Having these will make reporting any theft much easier.

Risks When Paying With Checks

Since paying with plastic comes with so many risks, you may be wondering whether to switch back to paper. The answer isn't so clear. While paying with cash is essentially identity-theft proof, carrying around wads of bills isn't exactly safe. And using checks can be even riskier than credit and debit cards. Still, millions of Americans use checks to pay their bills and make purchases. If you're one of them, take a few minutes to read about check fraud.

Identity thieves and other criminals may try to gain access to your checking account in a variety of ways, including:

- stealing a blank check or deposit slip from your home, purse, or vehicle
- stealing your account information while your check is awaiting transfer or is in transit between a merchant and the bank (an inside job by an unscrupulous employee or driver)

- searching for a canceled or old check in your trash, or
- going into your mailbox and removing a check you're sending to pay a bill, or a newly delivered box of blank checks.

Once a thief has an actual check of yours, it's no trick to make it payable to him or herself or even use your account numbers to make counterfeit checks in your name. Sometimes a color photocopy machine is all the thief needs. Even a checkbook from an old, closed account is useful to a thief, who may get away with writing many checks on it before getting caught.

A thief who is able to get additional personal information, such as your Social Security number, may be able to take over the account, transferring it to his or her address, or to open a new checking account in your name and write checks against it. Even if there's no money in the account, it could be a while before the duped recipients find out—and you could be the one facing arrest for writing bad checks.

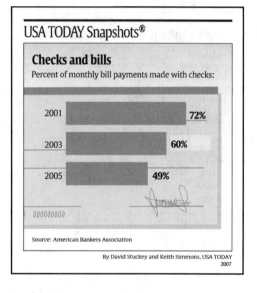

USA TODAY Snapshots®

Checks and bills

Percent of monthly bill payments made with checks:

2001   72%
2003   60%
2005   49%

Source: American Bankers Association

By David Stuckey and Keith Simmons, USA TODAY 2007

As online pay-by-check becomes more common, so too do the opportunities for the bad guys to use your information. To arrange a fraudulent online payment by check, all the thief needs is the account information on the front of your check—your bank routing number and account number. Once processed, the funds will be debited from your account and you'll learn about it only if you carefully read your next bank statement.

Your Financial Consequences After Check Fraud

If an identity thief cleans out your checking account, the path to getting your money back may be more complicated than just contesting a charge on your credit card. Laws stipulate who is on the hook—the bank or the consumer—in most instances of check fraud. It's rare that you'll end up suffering a financial loss for legitimate fraud. But banks hold a lot of power in making your life easy or difficult as you try to prove your innocence. It's always a good idea to pay attention to a bank's fraud policies and practices when you open up a new checking account.

No one knows how much money customers have lost from check fraud. But in 2007, banks alone lost $271 million from fake checks—a 160% increase from three years earlier, according to the American Bankers Association.

Even if the fraud wasn't your fault, you may face the consequences of bouncing a check, most likely a fee. In addition, your name may be reported to the ChexSystems network, a national database that alerts banks and lenders that potential borrowers pose a credit risk. If this happens, you'll have a hard time opening up a checking account, taking out a loan, or even renting an apartment.

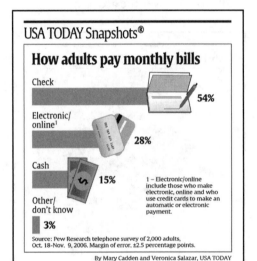

USA TODAY Snapshots®

How adults pay monthly bills

Check — 54%

Electronic/online[1] — 28%

Cash — 15%

1 – Electronic/online include those who make electronic, online and who use credit cards to make an automatic or electronic payment.

Other/don't know — 3%

Source: Pew Research telephone survey of 2,000 adults, Oct. 18–Nov. 9, 2006. Margin of error. ±2.5 percentage points.

By Mary Cadden and Veronica Salazar, USA TODAY 2007

Fraudsters Take Advantage of Check-Cashing Laws

Jill and Steven Parker's graduate school education didn't keep them from being fleeced of $22,000 after they advertised an apartment rental online. Susan Jones was taken in by a man she met online who used his charm and good looks to persuade her to send counterfeit checks to his so-called business associates.

And Rebecca Woodworth says her sister lost hundreds of thousands of dollars—and eventually committed suicide—after a fraudster convinced her she'd won a sweepstakes and just had to pay the taxes and fees on the winnings.

These stories have one thing in common: The fraudsters used a quirk in the check-cashing system to bilk consumers.

Banks are required to make funds available to customers within a few days of when the check is deposited—even if the check has yet to clear. This law was enacted in the 1980s after consumers complained that banks were holding onto deposits for inordinate amounts of time.

The law has, indeed, allowed consumers to access their money more quickly. But it's also provided another avenue for fraud. In a dizzying variety of check scams, fraudsters are sending out checks to consumers and urging them to cash them and wire some of the proceeds back. Because the money appears quickly in consumers' bank accounts, they assume the check has cleared. It's only later—often after they've already wired money to scamsters—that consumers learn that the check is counterfeit.

The most important advice is also the simplest: Be extra careful about depositing checks and wiring money to people you don't know. And never accept a check for more than the amount of an item you're selling.

"There's no legitimate reason for someone to write you a check and then ask you to wire money back to them," says Susan Grant, director of the fraud center at the National Consumers League, a consumer advocacy group.

Fraudsters Take Advantage of Check-Cashing Laws, cont'd

Many people don't realize, Grant says, that even though the money appears in their account, it could take weeks for the check to be processed. By the time they realize the check is a fake, they may already have wired money to the fraudsters.

It doesn't help that some banks are giving consumers questionable information. The Parkers, of Richmond, Virginia, say they lost $22,000 after their bank told them that a check they deposited had cleared, only to have that same check later bounce.

The check came from someone who had replied to an online ad the couple had posted about an apartment for rent. The prospective renter said his employer was transferring him to Chicago from the United Kingdom. He said his company would send the Parkers a $25,000 check that had been promised to him for moving expenses. The couple could deduct the first and last month's rent before wiring his agent any money left over.

After the couple deposited the check, they waited four or five days before calling the bank. They confirmed with two bank employees that the check had "cleared" and verified the funds were in their account. After taking these precautions, they transferred $22,000 back to the prospective renter's agent.

The call from the bank came a few days later. The check had bounced. "This happened two weeks before Christmas, and we were devastated," Jill says.

Her bank told her it wasn't liable for the loss.

Nessa Feddis, senior federal counsel at the American Bankers Association, says banks have no "legal or common understanding of the word cleared." Some banks may consider a check to clear when the consumer can access the funds; others might consider a check to clear only after it can no longer bounce.

"Con artists take advantage of check rules," by Kathy Chu, March 18, 2008.

Protecting Your Account From Check Fraud

Like plastic cards, checks can be useful and safe if you act carefully. Follow these tips to avoid becoming a victim of check fraud:

- **Never write your Social Security number on a check.** Merchants typically need your name, address, phone number, and driver's license number. But some are now requiring your Social Security number, as well. If a merchant requests this as a form of identification, just say no. It's much safer to shop somewhere else.

- **Don't leave anything behind at the checkout counter.** Make sure you retrieve your ID and receipt after your purchase.

- **Don't throw away blank checks or checks that you've made mistakes on.** Shred them before tossing them.

- **Write checks only to those you know and trust.** Because your check includes your bank routing number and account number, it makes it easier for thieves to access your bank account. Consider setting up electronic funds transfer payments for some bills.

- **Get a locking mailbox.** If you have a roadside mailbox, or one that thieves can reach into, it's time for an upgrade. Otherwise both your outgoing check payments and your incoming account information and new checks are vulnerable. In the meantime, try to remove mail from your mailbox soon after delivery. If you're not at home during the day, a trusted neighbor may agree to pick up your mail.

- **Don't keep a higher account balance than you need.** For people who are good at saving money, the checking account can be an accidental repository of your long-term savings. That's not only a bad financial move, given the interest you could be earning elsewhere, but it exposes your money to theft. Make a habit of viewing your balance and moving any amounts higher than you need for daily life to a less-accessible savings account, CD, or brokerage account.

- **After a home burglary, look for your checkbook.** Some thieves may steal only a single check, and use it to make or request more. Unless you're sure your checkbook and bank records went untouched, assume you're a victim and take the follow-up steps described in Chapter 11.

Despite your best efforts to prevent card or check fraud, you may still fall victim to these crimes. Fortunately, if you are victimized, there are steps you can take to minimize the damage, as described in Chapter 11.

Brokerage Accounts: Risks and Protective Measures

Most online brokerage or investment accounts, such as those offered by eTrade or Charles Schwab Corp., use stringent internal security systems and measures to protect your accounts. It's also more difficult to get money out of these types of accounts. Nevertheless, brokerage accounts are a prime target for identity thieves, because they typically hold more money than regular bank accounts. Some scammers will go the extra mile to gain access to your online brokerage accounts, in pursuit of the potentially high payoff.

As USA TODAY's Byron Acohido reported in 2007, "Cybercrooks can easily breach online brokerage accounts because most require just a username and password to access over the Internet. Stolen log-on data for online brokerage accounts is readily available on Internet chat channels and websites, called carding forums, where cybercriminals congregate. A typical price: 10% of the balance in the account, says Dan Clements, CEO of security firm CardCops."

While getting your money transferred from your brokerage account to an unauthorized bank account is tricky for such scammers, they have other ways of getting your money. For example, they might sell your investments and reinvest them in penny stocks they own to pump the value, then sell their holdings, leaving you with worthless shares. Thieves have used such tactics at Fidelity, Merrill Lynch, and Charles

Schwab in the past. Fortunately, while not legally responsible for reimbursing you, most brokerage firms will cover such fraud.

To prevent investment or brokerage account fraud, never respond to emails requesting your personal information, even if they appear to come from your investment company. Check your account statements regularly, even if you think there's nothing to look at because you haven't deposited or withdrawn any money lately. But never check your account statement on a public computer, which may be vulnerable to hackers. If the account comes with an ATM card, don't carry it around with you—carry only a card with access to your lower-balance accounts. Finally, keep your personal computer updated with the latest Internet security software (as described in Chapter 4) to ensure that your online transactions are secure.

USA TODAY Snapshots®

When is information on paper most at risk?

In a trash bin **62%**

In a communal printing tray **46%**

At an office desk **44%**

Awaiting disposal or shredding **31%**

Note: Multiple responses allowed

Source: Alliance for Secure Business Information survey of 819 workers. Margin of error ±4 percentage points

By Jae Yang and Veronica Salazar, USA TODAY 2008

Secure Your Online Presence

ost U.S. homes access the Internet through at least one computer—and an increasing number have a computer in every bedroom. These connections let you and your family pay bills, shop (without dropping), exchange emails, share photos, chat with friends and strangers, play online games, download favorite tunes, and much more.

The downside to all this connectedness is that it opens the door for online identity theft. Any online communication, whether it's surfing, email, instant messaging (IM), or social networking, increases your risk. Various online threats can lure you to unsecure websites, follow your movements, lurk behind the websites you visit, and steal or con you out of your personal information. Let's look at how to fight back.

USA TODAY Snapshots®

Biggest computer security concerns
What types of computer security issues does your organization face? Top responses:

Virus/worm — 70%
Lack of user awareness — 60%
Abuse by authorized users — 46%
Remote access — 45%
Browser-based attacks — 40%

Note: Multiple responses allowed
Source: CompTIA's Fourth Annual Benchmark Study, Committing to Security survey of 2,598 information technology professionals. Margin of error ±2 percentage points.

By Jae Yang and Julie Snider, USA TODAY 2006

Meet the Virtual Identity Thief

Online identity theft is considered easy and lucrative by thieves, and the newspapers are already full of cases to prove it.

Michael Dolan, for example, reportedly masterminded a phishing scam that targeted America Online (AOL) subscribers. Over the course of four years, Dolan and a group of hackers sent millions of email notices that appeared to come from legitimate sources, such as AOL's billing department, to trick members into providing their billing information. After stealing $400,000 from hundreds of unsuspecting AOL members, he was sentenced to seven years in prison.

Seventeen-year-old Owen Thor Walker was barely out of high school when he joined an international cybercrime ring that compromised more than one million computers and used them to steal nearly $20 million from private bank accounts. He was paid $31,000 to create software that allowed the crime ring to build a botnet—a large network of zombie computers that prey on users' Web vulnerabilities. The software, which New Zealand prosecutors described as the most advanced they'd seen, helped scammers steal credit card information and break into accounts. A judge dismissed the charges against Walker in 2008, saying that she didn't want to stifle a potentially bright future.

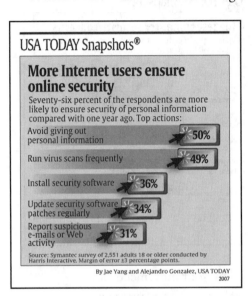

USA TODAY Snapshots®

More Internet users ensure online security

Seventy-six percent of the respondents are more likely to ensure security of personal information compared with one year ago. Top actions:

Avoid giving out personal information **50%**

Run virus scans frequently **49%**

Install security software **36%**

Update security software patches regularly **34%**

Report suspicious e-mails or Web activity **31%**

Source: Symantec survey of 2,551 adults 18 or older conducted by Harris Interactive. Margin of error ±3 percentage points.

By Jae Yang and Alejandro Gonzalez, USA TODAY 2007

These two online thieves got caught. But more are still out there, using common sense and an understanding of online commerce, Internet security, and simple human nature to trick online users. While their methods are different from other identity thieves, their goal is the same—to steal your personal information for their own fun and profit.

Online identity theft is not only being perpetrated by individual scammers, but also by large rings, many of which make money by selling your sensitive information on underground websites. One of the most well-known was Shadowcrew.com, an online marketplace with over 4,000 members. It trafficked in at least 1.5 million stolen credit and bank card numbers and stole over $4 million, mainly from credit and bank card issuers. Fortunately, Shadowcrew.com was shut down by the U.S. government a few years ago. But as soon as one such organization gets caught, another seems to pop up.

Today's virtual identity thief could be the shy geek next door or a highly skilled criminal mastermind. Chances are, you'll never find out. But these crooks have one thing in common—like most other predators, they will likely target easy marks. If you understand how they work and how to protect yourself, you can safely use the technologies they target without having your identity stolen.

Online World Resembles Wild, Wild West

The Internet today can be compared to the lawless Wild West, with a worldwide society of underground crime rings profiting from online identity theft. Cybercrime, which includes a broad range of offenses including viruses, bots, and phishing scams, is one of the fastest-growing crimes in the world. Fraudsters operate in a digital world that's largely beyond the reach of government and law enforcement agencies.

While the United States is still the source of the majority of malware, spam, and viruses in the world, rapidly developing countries, such as Russia and China, are catching up.

According to Iain Mulholland, former Security Strategist and Manager of the Microsoft Security Response Center at Microsoft, and now Chief Technology Officer of HauteSecure, a company that protects against malicious software, many online threats are caused by "script kiddies," or young teenagers looking for bragging rights.

But, "Today, a much more organized, underground criminal community is taking over," says Mulholland. "These bad guys are running their operations as businesses, employing conventional business techniques, using business cycles, and even launching marketing campaigns…think of it as the Russian mafia expanding into the online world."

Email Risks

Have you ever received an email asking you to click on a link or open an attachment to take advantage of a special offer? Cathy, a New Jersey mom, did, thus starting her identity theft horror story.

According to the message in Cathy's inbox, she needed to verify her eBay account information. She dutifully clicked the link (which led to a bogus eBay website) and provided her information. As a result, her personal data was sold on the black market to a member of a terrorist organization, which used stolen credit card numbers to pay for websites on computer hacking and bomb-making. The buyer of Cathy's information was eventually tracked down and prosecuted, but only after she spent years trying to undo the damage he'd done.

Let's look at some of the other ways that identity thieves use email to steal personal information from unsuspecting victims.

Spam

Anyone who uses email is almost guaranteed to get a lot of spam—that is, unsolicited, junk email from strangers. At best, spam is irritating and takes time to delete. At worst, it increases the number of emails coming your way from scam artists and identity thieves—most of them employing "phishing" scams, as described next. For how to reduce the amount of spam you receive, see "Use spam filters," below.

Phishing

Phishing is much like what it sounds like—identity thieves fishing for your personal information. Your Social Security number is the big catch, but they'll happily reel in smaller fry like your name, address, credit card details, and PIN codes.

A typical phishing scam starts with a scammer sending out millions of emails that appear to come from an established business, perhaps mimicking its brand, logo, and graphic design. The email might describe a problem with your account or order, or push a "special offer." In some (but not all) cases, the scam is made to look even more convincing by linking you to an actual website (phony, of course; mimicking legitimate websites is also known as "spoofing"). Having drawn you in, they then ask you for sensitive information or activate malicious code.

Many phishing emails appear to come from a trusted source, such as a friend or reputable company. In some cases, that's because scammers have found a way to infect your friend's computer with a malicious virus or worm. Or they mimic a real company's domain name by using a fake one that's deceptively similar: for example, "mircosoft.com" instead of "microsoft.com."

In Chapter 5, we'll discuss some of the different themes that come up in phishing scams in detail, but here's a taste of the possibilities. You may get an email claiming that your help is needed to access a large sum of money for a business deal, medical emergency, or other reason. Some scammers go so far as to pose as an old friend in need of urgent medical attention, pretending that the sender will die if you don't respond. Or the sender may promise a hefty reward in exchange for your help. But in reality, the object is just to trick you into revealing your financial information.

In another type of phishing scam, you might receive an email that appears to come from a major bank, warning you that recent fraud activity has jeopardized the security of your account. Alarmed, you quickly click the link that takes you to a fake—but very convincing looking—website, where you go ahead and enter your bank account number as requested. Any personal or financial information you enter is instantly in the hands of identity thieves.

Some phishing scams appear to come from government organizations, such as the Internal Revenue Service (IRS) or the Social Security Administration (SSA). Still other scammers try to trick you into believing that you are a lottery or contest winner, in the hopes that you'll hand over your information to claim your "prize."

If you're thinking, "They won't fool me," don't be so sure. True, some phishing efforts are full of misspellings and have "fake" written all over them, but the more sophisticated ones use tactics like:

- Using the names of real people who work at the company, such as CEOs or well-known executives, in the text of the message or in the "from" line. For example, in the infamous Nigerian Money scam, phishers may pose as real Nigerian government officials.

- Making a link in an email (and the spoofed website it redirects to) appear legitimate, for example by inserting a URL that's only slightly misspelled, a letter or two away from the real one. Or they might even show you a valid URL, which when you click it, takes you to a different, phony site. (To do this, scammers exploit vulnerabilities in a legitimate website, by which they can insert malicious code redirecting users.)

- Scaring you with urgent messages, for example warnings that you'll lose access to your financial accounts or be audited unless you respond immediately.

Sample Bank Phishing Message

Here's what a classic phishing message might look like—note the impersonal greeting ("Dear Bank Customer"), urgent request for a response, and Web address that's disturbingly close to the real thing.

Date: Sun, 13 July 2008 12:22:23

From: customerservice@abcbank.ca

Reply-to: upgrade17@googlemail.com

To: undisclosed-recipients

Subject: IMPORTANT ACCOUNT INFORMATION

Dear Bank Customer,

This is your official notification from ABC Bank. Your online account information has expired. If you want to continue using your online service, you must renew your online account with 24 hours. If not, your online account will be deleted. In order to activate your account confirm your identity at: http://www.abcbank-request.com.

Thank you,

Your ABC Bank Customer Service Team

Sample Delivery Company Phishing Message

Here's another clever phishing email, which boldly pretended to be from UPS (it's not), and included text to make it look as though Scott Mitic had originally inquired about a package delivery.

From: John Henry [mailto:johnhenry.support@ups.com]
Sent: Monday, September 15, 2008 9:12 AM
To: Scott Mitic
Subject: Re: missing package

Mr./Mrs. Scott Mitic

I am sorry for this late reply, but we have good news. We managed to track your package, and we have attached the invoice you asked for to this reply.

The invoice contains the correct tracking# , since the one you gave us was invalid. You can use it on the ups website to track your shipment.

Thank you

John Henry

UPS Customer Care Department

---On Mon, 9/08/08, Scott Mitic <scottmitic@trustedid.com> wrote:

From: Scott Mitic <scottmitic@trustedid.com>
Subject: missing package
To: support@ups.com
Date: Monday, September 8 , 2008, 10:38 AM

I have recently used UPS to send a package to my cousin but he never received it. Also, the tracking number doesn't check on the website, and I lost the invoice. Can you forward me a copy?
Here you have the tracking# : 03073332100016836200.

These clever tactics are paying off for phishers. The number of U.S. adults who believe they've received phishing emails nearly doubled between 2004 and 2006. Approximately 109 million U.S. adults received phishing emails in 2006, up from 57 million in 2004. And many of them fell for the ruse—leading to financial losses of more than $2.8 billion in 2006. (Source: Gartner Research, www.gartner.com.)

Unauthorized access to your email account

Someone who gains access to your email account can do a lot of damage—not only invade your privacy, but potentially find out where you bank and do business and gain access to your accounts.

For example, let's say you leave the Internet café PC where you'd been checking your email, and forget to clear your information (or worse, told the system you wanted it to remember your username and password for that computer). The next person who comes along looks like an ordinary type, but in fact has already marked you as a potential target. He gets right into your email and discovers your latest message from your online bank.

Although hacking into your bank account might take some work, he goes into some of your other accounts—like your photo-sharing account—and clicks the link for "I forgot my password." An email with your password soon arrives. And it just happens to be the same one you use for many of your online accounts—so now the thief can get to work.

USA TODAY Snapshots®

What actions should the U.S. government take to better safeguard cyberspace?

Establish better communication with and among the private sector	71%
Educate people about cybersecurity roles and capabilities	71%
Make cybersecurity a greater priority	70%
Educate critical infrastructures on cybersecurity risks and how to respond to cyberemergencies	68%

Note: Multiple responses allowed
1 – Oil & gas, nuclear, energy, water or other critical industries
Source: CSO magazine survey of 389 chief security officers and security executives.
Margin of error ±5 percentage points.

By Jae Yang and Sam Ward, USA TODAY
2006

As this example shows, some of the easiest ways to access your email account have nothing to do with high-tech hacking. You might provide the access yourself—and not just in public places. Leaving your address and password automatically entered on your work or home computer can also expose you to risk.

Web-Surfing Risks

Surfing the Web may feel like a private activity, but in fact you're exposing your computer to unwanted contact with anyone else who has a computer. All you have to do is visit a website or click a link and—voila—you're a victim! Here's a guide to some of the most common or virulent problems.

Malware

Malware is one of the biggest threats in the Internet today, and it comes in many shapes and forms. Malware means any program that infiltrates or damages your computer system without your consent, usually in order to steal your information or track your Web-surfing habits for financial gain or criminal purposes.

Malware can hijack your browser, redirect your search attempts, launch malicious pop-up ads, track your Web-surfing habits and entries, and cause your computer to become slow and unstable.

Your computer can get infected by malware in several ways. Often, it comes bundled with free, downloadable programs. (File-sharing programs, such as Kazaa and LimeWire, are among the biggest culprits.) Simply installing a free screensaver may be all it takes. Other malware installs itself by taking advantage of any vulnerabilities in your Web browser. In such a case, no action is required on your part—simply visiting the wrong Web page will lead to infection if your computer isn't adequately protected.

Any type of code or program that monitors and collects your personal information or damages your computer falls into the malware category. There are many types of malware, including adware, spyware, viruses, worms, and Trojan horses, all of which will be addressed in this section.

Adware

Adware is software that generates pop-up advertisements in the applications you use on your computer. Most adware programs track your computer usage in order to accurately target advertising to your interests and online behavior.

Adware is considered a fair tradeoff for people who don't want to pay for software. Many software developers today offer their applications as "sponsored" freeware to those who don't want to pay for it. You enjoy their software for free and they serve you random advertisements.

Usually the biggest concerns with adware are privacy and annoyance issues. But adware can also be used as a vehicle to install spyware, discussed next.

Spyware

Like adware, spyware is usually downloaded without your knowledge, as the result of an action you take (such as clicking on a pop-up). Its spying capabilities may include installing a "key logger" to monitor your keystrokes, scanning files on your hard drive, displaying ads to lure you to websites containing more malware, snooping your other applications such as chat programs, and more—all the while sending the information it finds back to the spyware's creator. Key loggers are particularly malicious, as they secretly track everything you do on the Internet, including everything you type (passwords, account numbers, and other valuable personal information).

Many spyware programs trick you into installing them. For example, a pop-up window could have a fake "close" button that actually downloads spyware when you click it. Or, a spyware program might sneak onto your system when you download a free application or peer-to-peer file-sharing product, such as LimeWire or Kazaa.

Viruses and worms

A computer virus is a type of malware that attaches itself to a program or file so that it can spread from one computer to another, infecting each vulnerable computer along the way. Like a human virus, some viruses are minor, while others cause major damage and inconvenience. For example, while some viruses simply cause your computer to slow down, others instruct your computer to send information to other systems (possibly owned by identity thieves) without your knowledge. The majority of viruses are spread via executable files, such as email attachments or images, meaning that you probably won't get infected by a virus unless you open a malicious file.

A worm is similar to a virus in that it spreads from one computer to another, but unlike a virus, it doesn't require a person to open an attachment. Rather, worms either exploit vulnerabilities (security holes) on your system or use a scam to trick you into executing them. Once executed, they take advantage of the built-in file-transport or information-transport features on your system, allowing them to travel without your consent or knowledge.

Both viruses and worms are self-replicating, meaning that they send out thousands of copies of themselves, rather than just a single copy. For example, a worm could send a copy of itself to everyone listed in your email address book. Then, it would replicate and send itself out to everyone listed in each recipient's address book, and so on.

Because viruses and worms copy themselves so many times, they tend to be extremely taxing on the systems they infect. If you've been infected by a virus or worm, you will likely notice that your computer has slowed down considerably. If after rebooting, it's still extremely sluggish, there's a good chance your machine has been compromised.

Trojan horses

Trojan horses are another type of malware, usually downloaded from the Internet, which looks innocent but carries hidden programs, commands, or script. The name comes from stories of the Trojan War, in which the Greeks presented a large wooden horse to their enemies, the Trojans, supposedly as a peace offering. After the horse was inside the Trojans' guarded city walls, Greek soldiers snuck out at night and opened the gates to the city, allowing their army to attack.

Like viruses, Trojan horses require you to take some type of action, such as opening a link or file you received via email or IM. For example, if someone emails you a link to what looks like an innocent game (for example, "Play the Winter Olympics now"), you'd have to download a small file to see the game. If the game included a Trojan horse, you'd also unknowingly download a malicious program that might not only take control of your email address list and send the infected link out to everyone on your list, but also create an access point on your computer that allows malicious users to control your system and potentially get at your confidential or personal information. Your friends will likely think you're sending them a cool game and click on it, too, perpetuating the scam. (The program can't self-replicate without fooling people into downloading it, but the fact that it ostensibly came from you may be enough to do just that.)

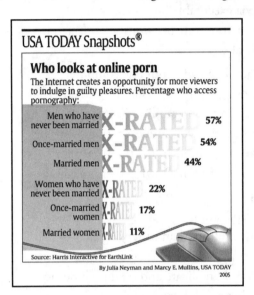

USA TODAY Snapshots®

Who looks at online porn
The Internet creates an opportunity for more viewers to indulge in guilty pleasures. Percentage who access pornography:

Men who have never been married — 57%
Once-married men — 54%
Married men — 44%
Women who have never been married — 22%
Once-married women — 17%
Married women — 11%

Source: Harris Interactive for EarthLink

By Julia Neyman and Marcy E. Mullins, USA TODAY 2005

Trojan horses are frequently included in videos or images. In 2008, the Oregon Department of Revenue notified 2,300 taxpayers that their names, addresses, or Social Security numbers may have been stolen by a Trojan horse program downloaded accidentally by a former worker who was surfing pornographic sites at work. The malicious program was designed to capture keystrokes on the former employee's computer. Because the employee was responsible for entering taxpayer name and address changes, as well as Social Security numbers, the Trojan horse was able to gather this data and send it to an unrelated website.

Infection by a Trojan horse is often indicated by abnormal activity on your computer system, such as programs being opened unexpectedly without any action by you, or repeated system crashes.

Bots and botnets

If someone told you your computer had been turned into a robot, you'd probably laugh. But certain types of malware allow an attacker to take control of a computer, which is then referred to as a "bot"—short for robot. The attacker then uses the bot to send out spam and phishing emails to other computers. Many of these attackers are large criminal organizations.

The takeover is usually engineered either via a phishing email or a worm that travels the Internet looking for vulnerable, unprotected computers to infect—that is, computers whose owners haven't installed the protective types of software described later in this chapter.

The bots are usually drawn into a larger network of infected machines, known as a "botnet," which may be made up of thousands of victim machines around the world. In fact, an estimated 11% of U.S. computers are affected by bots—in most cases without the owner's knowledge.

After infecting a machine, the bots report back to their master, but try to stay hidden until instructed to carry out a specific task. Their tasks might include installing spam, viruses, and spyware, and stealing sensitive information. Or your computer may send phishing emails to your friends and other contacts to perpetuate the scam.

For example, a few years ago, a criminal organization compromised the Southwest Vacations Web server, uploading a small piece of malicious code that redirected visitors to a phony site in China. Once users entered this phony site, their Web browsers were probed for vulnerabilities. If any were detected, the scammers gained control of users' computers and installed keystroke loggers to steal their passwords and other sensitive data.

Bots Bring Home the Bacon

At the height of his powers, Jeanson James Ancheta felt unstoppable. From his home, the then-19-year-old high school dropout controlled thousands of compromised PCs, or "bots," that helped him earn enough cash in 2004 and 2005 to drive a souped-up 1993 BMW and spend $600 a week on new clothes and car parts.

He once bragged to a protégé that hacking Internet-connected PCs was "easy, like slicing cheese," court records show.

But Ancheta got caught. In the first case of its kind, he pleaded guilty to federal charges of hijacking hundreds of thousands of computers and selling access to others to spread spam and launch Web attacks.

Ancheta proved more enterprising than most. He infected thousands of PCs and started a business—#botz4sale—on a private Internet chat area. From June to September 2004, he made about $3,000 on more than 30 sales of up to 10,000 bots at a time, according to court records.

By late 2004, he started a new venture, court records show. He signed up with two Internet marketing companies, LoudCash of Bellevue, Washington, and GammaCash Entertainment of Montreal, to distribute ads on commission.

But instead of setting up a website and asking visitors for permission to install ads—a common, legal practice—he used his bots to install adware on vulnerable Internet-connected PCs, court records show. Typically, payment for each piece of adware installed ranges from 20 cents to 70 cents.

Checks ranging as high as $7,996 began rolling in from the two marketing firms. In six months, Ancheta and his helper pulled in nearly $60,000, court records show.

During one online chat about installing adware, Ancheta advised his helper: "It's immoral, but the money makes it right."

 "Cybercrime, Inc.—Malicious-software spreaders get sneakier, more prevalent," by Byron Acohido and Jon Swartz, April 23, 2006.

Pharming

Pharming scams install malicious code on your personal computer or server that misdirects you to fraudulent websites without your knowledge or consent. You, acting responsibly, might type in a perfectly accurate URL for a legitimate company and be unwittingly taken to a look-alike site. Having no reason to doubt that you're dealing with your bank, for example, you might readily enter your credit card number, bank account number, or password.

Pharming is often described as "phishing without a lure," because no action is required on your part—the malicious code does the dirty work. You don't even need to click on an email link to become a victim. Pharming scams can be conducted in either of two ways:

1. **When you click on an emailed attachment, scammers launch malware that alters the host files on your computer.** Host files are the text files used by your operating system to store the Internet Protocol (IP) address of the sites you visit. (IP addresses are the true, numerical identifiers of every computer or network on the Internet, which you don't see because Web servers quietly translate them into more user-friendly domain names.) If a scammer alters a particular host file with the wrong IP address, you'll be redirected to a phony site even if you type the correct address into your browser window.

2. **Scammers exploit vulnerabilities in domain name system (DNS) servers.** DNS servers are computers that resolve a familiar address you type, such as "www.ebay.com," into their real IP addresses, which are usually something like "232.645.0.1." The pharmers inject phony information into them, which also redirect you to sites run by fraudsters. In this method of pharming, it's not necessary to corrupt individual personal computer host files. A scammer directly compromises a DNS server, which handles millions of Internet users' requests for URLs. You could end up at a bogus site without any warning signs of fraud. Fortunately, most DNS servers today have strong security mechanisms in place, but pharmers are constantly finding new ways to get around them.

Fight Off Wireless Pirates

According to Symantec and the Internet Education Foundation, 56 million Americans use wireless technology. And Symantec found that nearly 50% of wireless users in Houston, Los Angeles, New York, and Chicago "leave their doors wide open" to wireless pirates or wardrivers, who take advantage of the "free" bandwidth. How did the researchers figure this out? They actually played the part of wireless pirates, driving through neighborhoods with a wireless-enabled laptop looking for unsecured wireless networks. They found thousands of unsecured networks just waiting to be compromised.

The worst aspect of this problem is that some pirates hack in to steal personal information. They often use sniffers, which are malicious programs that steal passwords, credit card numbers, and other sensitive information.

If you have a wireless network in your home that isn't secured, you've greatly increased your risk of identity theft. To be safe, check the security instructions that come with your wireless access point. At a minimum, don't allow your access point to broadcast its name automatically—often referred to as the SSID (Service Set IDentifier). Additionally, set your access point to encrypt your wireless data using WEP (Wired Equivalency Privacy) technology. This will stop thieves from being able to easily see the data you are sending and receiving over your network.

Instant Messaging (IM) Risks

Because it's so easy to create an IM identity and chat with others, instant messaging is a popular target for online scams. Virtual thieves hack into accounts and impersonate legitimate users in order to trick other, unsuspecting IM users into giving up their personal data. Just like email attachments and links, IM file attachments and links can carry malicious viruses, worms, and Trojan horses used to conduct identity theft.

Picture this: You receive an IM containing a link from someone in your contact list, saying "OMG! Check this out. It is so funny!" The link appears to contain a JPEG photo file which, if clicked, asks you to save or run a file. Do you run the file?

If you say "yes," you might activate a malicious file that infects your computer with spyware, which can track everything you do online and report your activity (and possibly user names and passwords) back to the scammer who infected you. Of course, that scammer wasn't your friend at all. Some mass-mailing worms steal IM buddy lists (personal directories of friends and family) to use for phishing email distribution lists.

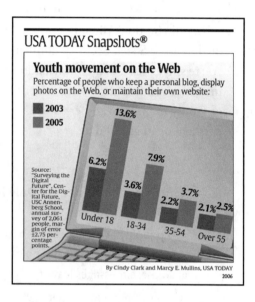

USA TODAY Snapshots®

Youth movement on the Web
Percentage of people who keep a personal blog, display photos on the Web, or maintain their own website:

■ 2003
■ 2005

13.6%
6.2%
7.9%
3.6%
3.7%
2.2%
2.1% 2.5%

Under 18   18-34   35-54   Over 55

Source: "Surveying the Digital Future", Center for the Digital Future, USC Annenberg School, annual survey of 2,061 people, margin of error ±2.75 percentage points.

By Cindy Clark and Marcy E. Mullins, USA TODAY
2006

Social Networking Risks

Most people exercise caution about revealing personal information in a public place or when surfing online. Yet many don't think twice before posting all kinds of intimate information on social networking sites, such as MySpace or Facebook. In fact, a whopping 74% of social networkers divulge personal information such as their email address, name, and birthday. On top of that, 83% of online users download unknown files from other people's profiles.

Virtual identity thieves are counting on this lack of caution. They look at user profiles for information with which to customize attacks known as "spear phishing." For example, a spear phisher may pose as one of your social-networking contacts or friends to create phony messages—perhaps inviting you to participate in a supposed lottery or school reunion—that then trick you into revealing more personal data, such as your credit card or phone number.

Even if you don't directly post vital personal information like your birth date or Social Security number on your social networking site, you're still at risk. Using information about your home, hobbies, interests, and friends, a virtual identity thief could impersonate a friend or family member or other source, convincing you to provide your personal or financial data.

Identity Theft Isn't the Only Internet Privacy Problem

Many people have a false sense of privacy when sending emails and instant messages, acting as if no one else will ever see them—but in reality, these messages leave trails.

Former Congressman Mark Foley (R-Fla.) learned this lesson after he was caught sending sexually explicit emails to underage House pages and was forced to resign. Miss New Jersey 2007, Amy Polumbo, found herself in a similar predicament. Shortly after she won her title, pageant officials received two packages containing embarrassing photos of Polumbo pulled from her Facebook page. The sender tried to blackmail Polumbo into relinquishing her crown.

While these cases didn't result in identity theft, they demonstrate how, every day, information that could damage our reputations and lives is collected and sold.

Protecting Yourself With Smart Online Behavior

While many of your daily online activities—such as banking and shopping—are very safe, by now you can see how one false move could have dire consequences for your personal and financial security. The following tips can help you avoid getting hooked by an online scam.

Use spam filters

Any email program you use will come with its own internal spam-filtering system. When you first activate your account, it may automatically configure the spam filter on a low setting, which will capture only the more obvious spam messages and move them to the junk folder.

Depending on your needs—and how good a job your program does at separating the spam from the real mail—you might want to modify the settings so that more junk messages are captured and separated from your primary inbox. (Look for a tab or button called "Options," or anything mentioning junk email or spam.)

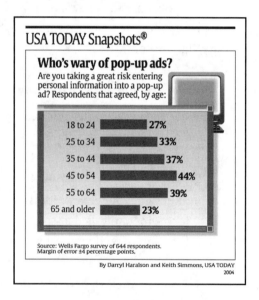

USA TODAY Snapshots®

Who's wary of pop-up ads?
Are you taking a great risk entering personal information into a pop-up ad? Respondents that agreed, by age:

Age	Percent
18 to 24	27%
25 to 34	33%
35 to 44	37%
45 to 54	44%
55 to 64	39%
65 and older	23%

Source: Wells Fargo survey of 644 respondents. Margin of error ±4 percentage points.

By Darryl Haralson and Keith Simmons, USA TODAY
2004

At the extreme, you could set your filters so that you receive messages only from addresses you've already identified as safe, while the rest are dumped into a separate junk mail box. The disadvantage to this is that you might forget to add some important contacts, and you won't see some legitimate messages, like those from old friends who got your email address from another friend, unless you regularly check your junk mail box.

You can also add individual contacts to the junk senders' list. For example, if you get junk mail from bogusbob@hotmail.com, you can add this email address to your junk senders' list. Conversely, you can tell your system that it was wrong in classifying an email as junk, and add the sender to your safe list.

Close unwanted pop-up ads the right way

You're already savvy enough not to open a suspicious pop-up ad, for example one saying that dangerous files have been found on your computer and you'd better click here right away. The trouble is, many people trying to close a pop-up mistakenly open it instead, potentially exposing their computer to malware or spyware. Always click on the "X" in the corner to close a pop-up. Whatever you do, don't click on any box within the pop-up window itself—even if that box beguilingly says "Ignore" or "Close."

Don't let the whole world know your email address

The more widely available your email address, the more it can be picked up and used by spammers and identity thieves to contact you. You can't guard your email address completely (friends may forward your messages to others, for example), but you can reduce its availability, as follows:

- **Don't put your email address on your website.** That's just asking for a program called a "spider" to find and harvest your address for spammers. If you really want your website visitors to be able to reach you, create a Web form for them to fill out.

- **Do your research before joining any online discussion list or forum.** See whether it posts participants' email addresses to the site for all to view. If so, tell the site administrator you won't be joining until they disguise the addresses to protect you from spammers.

- **Never reply to a spam email.** Not even to request being removed from the list. That just confirms that your address is an active, working one, guaranteeing you'll receive more mail.

- **Guard your friends' addresses, too.** Use "bcc" rather than "cc" when sending mass emails, so that people won't see each other's addresses. Also, don't fall for commercial sites' requests to "send this to a friend." And remove friends' addresses from email you forward. As this type of email etiquette catches on, your friends will hopefully learn to do the same for you.

Don't let in email invaders

Because email is a favorite method of access for so many scams, keeping your radar up about potentially suspicious emails is one of your most important lines of defense. This is especially true if the emails come from strangers. But a scam email can also come in the name of a friend, whose address the scammer is misusing. (Some people even get scam emails from their own email address!)

Be especially suspicious of any email with urgent requests for personal or financial information, such as your user names, passwords, credit card numbers, or Social Security number—even if it seems to come from your bank or a friend. Banks and e-retailers will never email you a request to input all of your sensitive information.

In fact, if you want to be extra careful, simply ignore any email from any financial institution. If the email appears to be legitimate, pick up the phone and call the sender—using the phone number on your bank statement or the back of your credit or ATM card—to independently verify the request, or log onto the website directly by typing in the Web address in your browser. And just in case that address is being secretly redirected in a pharming

USA TODAY Snapshots®

Library connections

How widely public libraries offer computer and Internet resources:

Offer access to database subscriptions (such as ancestry.com or World Book encyclopedia)	85.6%
Offer online homework resources	68.1%
Offer virtual reference	57.7%
Offer e-books	38.3%
Offer downloadable audio (such as podcasts and audiobooks)	38%

Sources: American Library Association, Libraries Connect Communities: Public Library Funding & Technology Access Study 2006-2007

By Michelle Healy and Adrienne Lewis, USA TODAY
2008

scam, check whether the site has an electronic certificate from a trusted Certificate Authority (CA), such as Versign (visit www.verisign.com to see the logo).

If you receive a pop-up that warns you of an invalid server certificate, especially when you're trying to conduct an online transaction, carefully review the certificate before entering any personal information. If the name on the certificate doesn't match the site you're attempting to reach, leave the site immediately.

To further protect against pharming, be sure to regularly update your antivirus and antispyware programs (as described below).

Never open email attachments or click on images and links unless you know who sent them and what they contain. Malware can be hidden in any of these. Even messages that appear to come from your good friends can be dangerous, especially if your friends' computers have been infected with malware that is now sending emails in their names. For example, many phishers send greeting cards that appear to come from people in your address book. Your best defense is to validate email attachments and links before opening them. Ask yourself questions like: Do I know for sure that this attachment was sent by my friend? Why would this person be sending me a holiday card for the first time in five years? Pick up the phone and call your friend if you have any doubts. You should also have all email attachments scanned by a reputable Internet security software program before opening (most do this automatically).

Be alert for signs of infection

While there are several different types of malware, most exhibit similar warning signs when you've been infected. Here are some of the most common red flags:

- Your computer is unusually slow.
- Your software displays error messages.
- Your computer won't shut down or restart.

- You see a lot more pop-up ads—sometimes even when you're not surfing the Web.

- Your computer launches programs or Web pages without your instruction, or does other weird things like open and close the CD tray.

If you experience any of these warning signs, don't panic. Here's what you need to do:

- Disconnect your computer from the Internet. Stop doing any online shopping, banking, or other activities that require passwords or other sensitive information (in case malware is sending your personal information to scammers).

- Reboot your computer.

- Back up your important data to an external drive (such as a CD or flash memory card). For more detailed instructions on backing up data on a PC, visit www.microsoft.com and conduct a search for "back up your data." To back up data on a Mac, visit http:// support.apple.com/kb/HT1553.

- Immediately install or update your Internet security software. Security software generally works for a specified time (like one year) unless you pay a renewal fee. Your software protects against the newest threats only if you keep it up to date.

- Allow your security software to conduct a full system scan. Delete everything the scanner identifies as a problem.

If malware is found, your security solution should offer recommendations for dealing with infected objects. If you experience any problems when following the steps above, contact your Internet security software vendor or, if that doesn't do it, get professional help. Now would be a good time to take advantage of any warranty that came with your computer offering free technical support. Another option is to reach out to a computer support company, such as Best Buy's Geek Squad. Also, many computer security companies, such as McAfee and Symantec, now offer customized, remote technical support from their websites at reasonable prices.

Instant message wisely

When using IM, there are a few things you can do to make sure you're safe. First, use a strong password (as described below) and change it often. And make sure your IM profiles don't contain personal information—especially phone numbers, addresses, pictures, or anything that could connect you or your family with your IM identities. Also use an antivirus program that automatically scans IM attachments.

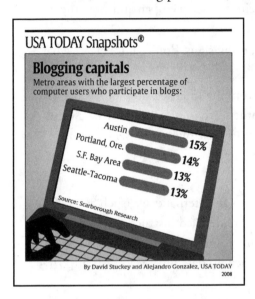

USA TODAY Snapshots®

Blogging capitals
Metro areas with the largest percentage of computer users who participate in blogs:

Austin — 15%
Portland, Ore. — 14%
S.F. Bay Area — 13%
Seattle-Tacoma — 13%

Source: Scarborough Research

By David Stuckey and Alejandro Gonzalez, USA TODAY
2008

Never open an IM attachment unless you've verified that it came from someone you know and trust. Even then, save the attachment to disk and then check it with an up-to-date virus scanner before opening the file. If your antivirus software has real-time protection, it will do this for you (check the features to make sure).

Social network with care

Social networking sites provide great opportunities for people to meet and share experiences. But to minimize the risk of becoming a victim, here are a few simple rules:

- **Limit your circle of contacts.** Consider restricting access to your page to a select group of people and setting your profile to "private" to prevent uninvited members from viewing your personal information.

- **Think twice before clicking a link or downloading a file.** Scam artists often post links to infected ad banners in their profiles. Avoid opening links or downloads from strangers, and never enter your password or account number unless you've verified the site's authenticity. When in doubt, always call the site owner to confirm.

- **Don't overshare personal information.** Identity thieves can easily find enough personal information on social networking sites to steal your identity. Especially avoid posting your full name, any financial data, your Social Security number, street address, birth date, or phone number.

Choose strong passwords and keep them safe

Think of your passwords as virtual keys that unlock the door to the private information stored on your computer and in your online accounts. You wouldn't use the same, easily copied key to open your front door, car, and office, right? That's why it's important to:

- **Select a password that's difficult to guess.** The first potential passwords a would-be identity thief will try are your name, your significant other or pet's name, and your place of birth. Better to at least go with your favorite nephew's dog's name.

- **Combine letters, numbers, and symbols.** The more characters in your password, the harder it is to guess. So instead of Bowser, make it Bowser!, or even Bow5erdog.

- **Store your passwords in a safe place.** Avoid storing them in cellular phones, handheld devices, or sticky notes taped to a computer or keyboard. One safe (albeit inconvenient) solution is to copy them onto a removable disk and store it in a locked drawer or file cabinet.

- **Don't use the same password for every service you use online.** All the thief would need to do is find one password and the code will have been cracked for all your accounts.

- **Change passwords on a regular basis, at least every 90 days.** This may seem like a hassle, but it can limit the damage caused by a thief who has already gained access to your account. Invest in password software if you need help managing your usernames and passwords. Password software saves your log-in names and passwords securely on your computer, allowing you easy access to all your passwords. All you have to do is remember one password—the one for your password software.

Look for security symbols on websites you visit

When submitting personal or financial information online, always double check that the site is secure. Even if the site's address begins with "https//," it may not be a guarantee. Phishers can spoof both the "https://" and yellow padlock icon used by secure Web servers, so be sure to enter the address of any banking or e-commerce website in your browser. And, to back that up by preventing pharming attacks, your best defense is to arm your computer with the right tools. Let's look next at how you can do so.

Who'd be careless enough to use the same password for all online accounts?

Actually, 9% of the American public, according to a survey by Consumer Reports.

Arming Your Computer for the Online Battle

With a little technical advice and common sense, it's not hard to prevent online identity theft. Virtual identity thieves want to make money as quickly and easily as possible. If you make their job difficult, they'll typically just move on to a more tempting target. Securing your computer is one of the most important things you can do to safeguard not just your identity, but everything on your computer.

Load security software

Internet security software is a must for anyone with an Internet connection. At a minimum, you want a security solution that includes antivirus, antimalware, identity protection, and a good firewall.

Antivirus software monitors online activities, such as email messages and Web browsing, in an attempt to block viruses, worms, Trojan horses, and other malicious threats from infiltrating your computer. Many Internet security programs include antispyware and antiadware protection, as well. Other "privacy suites" and similar products can help, but aren't necessary.

A firewall is your machine's first line of defense, as it controls who and what can communicate with your computer when you're online. It allows only those communications that it deems safe, and blocks "bad" traffic, such as viruses, worms, and other forms of malware.

Most people buy software from a local retailer or from the Internet (such as from BitDefender, MacAfee, Norton, TrendMicro, or Kaspersky). Look for programs that are easy to use, offer automatic updates, and are constantly updated with the free patches that fix newly discovered problems. A recent trend in computer security software is known as "heuristic" protection, which looks for general activity on your computer that may indicate risk of infection, rather than a specific virus "signatures" or markers that are absolute proof of an infection.

Also check into return policies and warranties, and keep all receipts for your records. When you order online, be sure the website you're ordering from is secure (see Chapter 6 for safe shopping tips).

Be sure your security software is configured to update itself every time you go online, so that you don't miss out on protection against the latest viruses. The brands listed above will automatically keep the software current as long as an Internet connection is available.

It is important that your security software be configured to automatically scan your computer on a regular basis (daily is ideal). Many computers that are infected by viruses appear to be virus-free, so you need an antivirus program that performs automatic scans of your entire computer regularly. Your software should also "clean out" any viruses and other threats it detects. Some brands detect malicious threats but don't actually get rid of them. You're better off choosing a brand that rids your computer of any threats it finds. Symantec, BitDefender, McAfee, and TrendMicro are a few of the well-known brands that both detect and destroy.

Does everyone else have a security patch?

Probably not. An estimated 40% of Internet users have not downloaded security patches to their Web browsers, resulting in more than 600 million users surfing the Web with a potentially unsafe browser.

Finally, make sure you update your software with whatever automatic updates your company recommends—don't delay, don't linger. Your software vendor's user manual will provide detailed instructions on any additional steps you may need to take.

Free Security Check-Up

Most computer security vendors offer free computer security checks for your computer. Visit the sites below to check your computer for known viruses, spyware, and more. Whether you're buying Internet security software for the first time or looking to upgrade what you already have, these sites can help you determine your Internet security needs by recommending an optimal level of protection.

- Symantec: http://security.symantec.com/sscv6/default. asp?langid=ie&venid=sym
- McAfee: http://us.mcafee.com/root/mfs/default.asp
- TrendMicro: http://housecall.trendmicro.com/us/index.html.

Update your computer with the latest security patches

One of the best ways to prevent online attacks is to apply patches and other software fixes as soon as they're offered. Security patches are updates that eliminate vulnerabilities that, when exploited, will compromise your computer or Web browser. These updates are issued for operating systems, software, and Web browsers. They make it much more difficult for online fraudsters to access your system, and block automated attacks (such as those sent via bots).

More recent versions of Microsoft Windows and popular security software can be easily configured to download and apply updates automatically so that you don't have to keep track of the latest software updates. Simply turn on the "auto-update" option in your software (your vendor's user manual will tell you where to find it).

When keeping your system safe and up to date, don't forget your browser. Make sure you're not surfing the Web unprotected, by regularly downloading the latest security patches, operating system updates, and virus definitions. Your security software may do this automatically, but if not, you'll have to do it yourself. For example, Internet Explorer or Firefox users should immediately download the latest Microsoft security upgrades and patches when they become available. Most vendors will alert you that an update is available when you launch their browsers. For more information and tutorials on how to update various browsers, visit http://security.getnetwise.org/tips/autoupdate.

Make sure your new computer is configured securely

If you've just purchased a brand-new computer, you probably assume that it has the latest and greatest security features. However, your new computer may have too little—or in some cases, too much—security for what you need to do. Even if you have Internet security software, make sure your computer and Internet browser security settings provide an additional layer of protection.

Your computer has numerous security settings that you can use, for example, to set a password policy so that all users who access your computer must change their password every 90 days. You can also set your computer to automatically check for high-priority updates that help protect against attacks. Your operating system's user guide provides details on how to alter your security settings.

Your Web browser (such as Internet Explorer or Firefox) also has predefined security levels that you can select. For example, you can use these settings to tell your browser whether or not to accept cookies, which are text files stored on your computer that help a website remember who you are and what you did on that site. Cookies are the reason that sites like Amazon and Google remember your name and preferred language and present you with targeted ads or product recommendations when you enter from your usual computer. Without cookies, you may have to reset your preferences every time you log on. If you want to accept cookies from selected companies and block cookies from all other sites, you can do so.

Cookies and pop-ups can make your life easier, but in some cases may increase your chances of being attacked. For example, while most cookies are safe, if a fraudulent website installs a cookie on your computer, the owner of that website can track every move you make online and use that information to conduct phishing or other identity theft scams.

It's best to adopt the highest level of security possible for your needs, instruct your browser to inform you if a site you're visiting is a suspicious one, and enable optional features, such as cookies or pop-ups, only when you need them. For example, you may need to enable pop-ups on certain sites to view discussion postings, quiz windows, videos, or download links.

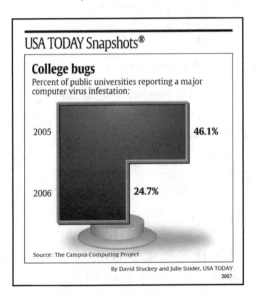

USA TODAY Snapshots®

College bugs
Percent of public universities reporting a major computer virus infestation:

2005 — 46.1%

2006 — 24.7%

Source: The Campus Computing Project

By David Stuckey and Julie Snider, USA TODAY 2007

But don't go overboard with strong security settings. For example, you probably don't want to have to approve every site you try to open, which would be time-consuming and just plain annoying. And you'll find that restricting certain features will limit some Web pages from loading or functioning properly.

Each browser is different, so you may have to search for the settings to change your level of security. For example, in Internet Explorer, you'd click "Tools" on your menu bar, select "Internet Options," choose the "Security" tab, and click the "Custom Level" button. However, in Firefox, you click "Tools" on the menu bar and select "Options." You may need to play around with the menu options, carefully read the instructions, or contact the vendor for help. Visit www.google.com/cookies.html for more instructions on how to change your cookie settings. Visit http://kb.iu.edu/data/atdz.html for instructions on how to change your pop-up settings.

Spot ID Theft Scams Before They Spot You

You've seen them. You've heard about them. Perhaps you've even fallen for one of them. Identity theft scams come in many forms, ranging from the eye-rollingly obvious to the highly polished and sophisticated.

You may not have to look far to encounter an identity theft scam. On any given day, you may get a phone message from an impostor claiming to be an IRS agent or a political survey-taker. Or you may get an email from a con artist saying you've won a contest or lottery, or a letter from someone hoping to take advantage of your good heart with urgent pleas to supposedly help victims of natural disasters or war. While the methods are different, the goal is the same: to obtain your personal information to commit identity theft.

USA TODAY Snapshots®

Internet is source of most fraud complaints

In addition to 246,570 identity theft complaints, there were 388,603 consumer fraud complaints reported. More than half were Internet-related:

Internet related **53%**

Other **47%**

Source: Federal Trade Commission's Consumer Sentinel database (complaints lodged by numerous law enforcement agencies in the USA, Canada and Australia)

By Shannon Reilly and Alejandro Gonzalez, USA TODAY 2005

The Federal Trade Commission (FTC) says that about 30.2 million adults—or 13.5% of the adult population—are scammed by fraudsters every year. That number continues to rise as new technologies are created and identity thieves come up with new ways to steal your sensitive information and hard-earned cash.

In this chapter, you'll be introduced to six of the top scams that criminals are using to get ahold of people's sensitive information. Better yet, you'll learn how to spot similar scams and prevent them from claiming you as a victim.

How Are Fraudulent Offers Pitched?

In 2007, the Federal Trade Commission (FTC) reported on how fraudsters usually contact or find their victims:

- In 27% of incidents, victims received fraudulent offers through print advertising—direct mail (including catalogs), newspaper and magazine ads, and posters and flyers.
- In 22% of incidents, the Internet (general websites, Internet auction sites, and email) was the fraudsters' medium.
- Television or radio advertising accounted for 21% of fraud incidents.
- Telemarketers pushed fraudulent products or services in the remaining 9% of cases.

Foreign Money Offer Scams

A variety of foreign money scams are designed to convince you to provide cash—or enough personal information with which to get at your cash—in return for supposed financial benefits or the chance to help someone in need. For example, you may receive letters or emails asking you to help get an inheritance out of a foreign country; bail out a friend in trouble (whose hotel has mysteriously lost telephone access); receive a shipment of goods; execute a real estate deal; or, in the most common scam, transfer money out of Nigeria.

The Nigerian money offer scam (also known as advance fee fraud or "4-1-9" fraud, after the relevant section of the Nigerian penal code) has been around for quite a few years, but still fools many victims. The Financial Crimes Division of the Secret Service reportedly receives about 100 telephone calls and 500 pieces of related correspondence each day about this scam, which bilks victims out of millions of dollars every year.

Here's how it usually works: You open your email inbox and find a legitimate-looking email from a Nigerian government official saying he urgently needs to transfer several thousands or even millions of dollars out of his country. He promises to pay you 25% of the transferred amount if you'll let him temporarily park the money in your bank account. But you're told that you'll need to act quickly in order to participate in this once-in-a-lifetime, lucrative opportunity.

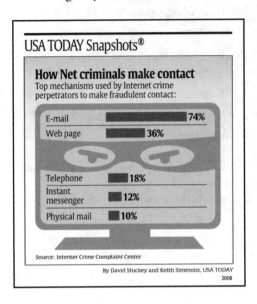

USA TODAY Snapshots®

How Net criminals make contact
Top mechanisms used by Internet crime perpetrators to make fraudulent contact:

E-mail 74%
Web page 36%
Telephone 18%
Instant messenger 12%
Physical mail 10%

Source: Internet Crime Complaint Center

By David Stuckey and Keith Simmons, USA TODAY 2008

While you might normally question the legitimacy of such an offer, you may lower your guard at seeing the high-quality forgeries of Nigerian government documents either attached in the email or sent to your home (if you provide your address). No mere amateur production, these may come with letterheads, government seals, or contracts. Some scammers have gone so far as to arrange meetings between victims and fake government officials in real or fake government offices. Others send forged checks as an advance on your "commission."

To accept, all you're asked to do is send your personal and bank information, business letterhead (if you have one), telephone, and fax numbers. As soon as you do, you're informed that there's a glitch in the execution of the transfer. If you don't provide further details of your bank account, you'll be pressured or threatened to provide large sums of money to ensure that the deal goes through. For example, a supposed official will tell you that an unforeseen tax or transfer fee to the Nigerian government needs to be paid before you receive the money.

Before you know it, your bank account has been drained, the "official" disappears, and you never receive the money you were promised. Months later, you may discover that someone has used your personal or account information to take out loans or commit other types of identity theft.

The following clues can help you detect the majority of money offer scams, whether from Nigeria or elsewhere:

- You're urged to respond immediately and confidentially.
- The sender claims to have strong ties to foreign government officials.
- Alternately, the sender claims to be someone in urgent need (a friend, family member, refugee, starving child—the list goes on).
- You're required to send your personal information or bank account details in order to participate.
- You're sent official-looking documents (forged, of course).
- You're told that you've been singled out (perhaps based on a personal recommendation) to participate in this once-in-a-lifetime opportunity (scammers actually send these messages to millions of people every day).
- You're promised huge returns for a simple task.
- You're asked to pay fees to move the transaction along.

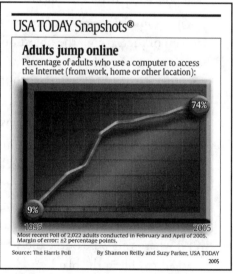

USA TODAY Snapshots®

Adults jump online
Percentage of adults who use a computer to access the Internet (from work, home or other location):

74%

9%

1995   2005

Most recent Poll of 2,022 adults conducted in February and April of 2005. Margin of error: ±2 percentage points.

Source: The Harris Poll   By Shannon Reilly and Suzy Parker, USA TODAY
2005

Just knowing how these schemes work is an important step in making sure you aren't taken in by one. Here are a few more precautions you can take:

- If you receive suspicious email, snail mail, phone calls, or faxes from Nigeria or any other country, do not respond, even to request more information. If it's supposedly from a friend, find a way to contact them without using the reply information given.

- Never, under any circumstances, travel to any meeting in response to an unsolicited offer. You won't see your money, and you could end up in physical danger.
- Report any suspicious offers you receive to the fraud department of your local police.

Fake Survey Scams, or "Pretexting"

Have you ever gotten a call asking you to take part in a survey? If you chose to participate, you were probably asked a series of seemingly harmless questions, such as the name of your cell phone or Internet provider, your pet's name, or your bank. Or maybe the caller claimed to be from your bank, wanted to verify an account transfer; or from the local police department, concerned about a call made on your line.

While some surveyors are the real thing, you may also have been a victim of pretexting. The object of this scam is to get your Social Security number, telephone records, bank or credit card numbers, or any other personal information, under false pretenses. By providing a credible "pretext" for why your private information is needed, pretexters can become successful identity thieves.

Pretexters put an impressive amount of effort into their work. Many conduct thorough background checks on their victims, scouring public records to get enough information to sound credible. Before a pretexter even dials your number, he or she might already know your family members' names, phone numbers, and addresses, as well as where you work, where you were born, and whether you own or rent. You'll simply be asked to "fill in the blanks."

For example, if a thief knows that you work at MTV and just bought a house in Los Angeles, he or she may pretend to be a human resources agent at MTV and offer you a special employee offer for new homeowners. Simply verify your bank account and Social Security number and you can take advantage of this special offer, promises the scammer.

In many cases, once a pretexter knows which bank or phone company you use, along with your SSN, it's easy to hack into your account by figuring out your password. And that's no trick if, like many people, you simply use your child or pet's name as a password—which you may have already revealed during that "survey." Other pretexters don't use the information themselves, but sell it to other shady operators.

How are you supposed to distinguish pretexters from legitimate businesses or organizations? Here are a few tips:

- **Verify first.** Never give out your personal information unless you've made sure the requestor is legitimate—most likely by hanging up and calling back the company's representatives at the phone number you have on file, or one from the phone book or Web.

- **Ask yourself why the caller doesn't already have the information on file.** Organizations with which you already do business will already have all the personal data they need about you. And they'll never ask you to reveal this data over the phone (or by email). Be especially suspicious if anyone asks for your SSN, mother's maiden name, pet or child's name, bank, brokerage, and credit card account numbers, or service provider (Internet, cable, phone, and so forth).

- **Don't leave personal information or financial statements lying around your home or work.** A pretexter who calls your family or coworkers might convince one of them to look for information on your files or bills.

- **Be informed.** Ask your financial institutions for their policies about sharing your information and what they're doing to prevent pretexting.

- **If you can't resist answering surveys, use common sense.** Never give out any financial or other information that could be sold or used by pretexters.

Vishing Scams

Using the phone to trick victims into releasing personal and financial data—a technique known as "vishing" (or voice phishing)—is one of the latest forms of identity theft. Not to be confused with basic phishing scams (described in Chapter 4), vishing uses Voice-over Internet Protocol (VoIP) to con people into divulging their personal and financial information.

Vishing scams are conducted in one of two ways. You may receive an email that appears to come from your bank or credit card company, instructing you to dial a phone number to confirm your account details. Or you may receive a recorded phone message asking you to call a toll-free number; at which point an automated answering service will request your account number, password, or Social Security number. In either case, the phone number belongs to an identity thief rather than a financial institution.

Vishing mimics the legitimate ways people interact with their financial institutions, so victims are more likely to respond. Many people mistakenly think that phone transactions are more trustworthy than Internet ones, due to the traceability and high cost of phone fraud. However, new VoIP services make it cheap and easy to obtain an anonymous account. Also, thieves can use software to create interactive voice response systems that sound exactly like banks or credit card companies.

In some cases, vishers already know your credit card number or other information about you, increasing the perception of legitimacy. Don't fall for it. For example, if they have your credit card number, they may ask you to "verify" the three-digit security code on the back of the card. Many sites require this code to make purchases. Once the thieves get your code, they've got what they need to go shopping on your dime.

To protect yourself from vishing, you can use some of the same techniques you'd use to avoid phishing scams:

- **Keep your guard up.** Always be highly suspicious when anyone asks for your credit card or bank numbers.

- **Before giving away any information, contact your bank or credit card company directly.** Ask them to verify the validity of an email or phone message.

- **Verify first.** For example, if something seems strange, ask the company to verify and provide details on a recent transaction you've made. A con artist is unlikely to have access to this type of information.

- **Tell your friends and family about this new scam.** People become victims of vishing scams mostly because they've never heard of this crime.

Expired Car Warranty Scams

Does your stomach clench at the thought of experiencing sudden car trouble and finding out your automobile warranty has expired, leaving you on the hook for big expenses? (Do you even know when your car warranty will expire?) Banking on this common fear, identity thieves have come up with the expired car warranty scam.

Identity thieves may contact you by telephone, email, or snail mail, "alerting" you that your car warranty is about to expire. In most cases, they'll say it's urgent that you respond immediately to keep your car under warranty or to reinstate your coverage. They'll also offer you a seemingly great deal to renew. If the offer sounds too good to be true, it probably is.

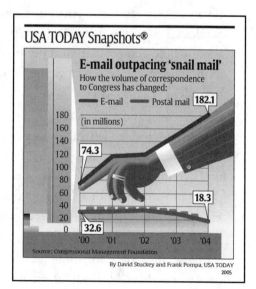

USA TODAY Snapshots®

E-mail outpacing 'snail mail'
How the volume of correspondence to Congress has changed:
━━ E-mail ━━ Postal mail 182.1
(in millions)
74.3
18.3
32.6
180 160 140 120 100 80 60 40 20 0
'00 '01 '02 '03 '04
Source: Congressional Management Foundation

By David Stuckey and Frank Pompa, USA TODAY
2005

If you respond, these crafty scammers will try to convince you to reveal your personal and financial information as part of supposedly renewing your warranty. They are often trolling for personal information, such as your Social Security number, address, date of birth, or credit card details.

If anyone contacts offering to sell you a car warranty, here's how to make sure you're not taken for a ride:

- **Verify first.** Never reveal personal financial information like your bank account number or SSN over the phone or via email or snail mail, unless you've first verified the company's legitimacy.

- **Review your original paperwork.** Check to see whether you already have a car warranty, or if your warranty has already expired. Many people who've received these offers say that their warranty had several more months on it or had expired a long time ago.

- **Get it in writing.** When considering an extended warranty, always get information in writing before you hand over any information or money.

Tax Scams

If you were to receive an email or phone call from the Internal Revenue Service (IRS) saying that your tax return had been selected for an audit, would you provide your personal information? If you answer yes, chances are you'd become a victim of identity theft.

Some of the biggest tax scams are "phishing" schemes, designed to steal personal and financial information via the Internet. In 2007, the Treasury Inspector General for Tax Administration identified at least 20 fake websites pretending to be the official IRS website. The IRS says that dozens of scams are reported each tax season. In 2006, even the commissioner of the New York State Department of Taxation and Finance, Andrew Eristoff, received a tax-related phishing email—on his government computer, no less.

In one common scam, an official-looking email informs you that you need to provide additional information before your tax return can be processed. The email directs you to a website displaying the IRS name and logo, where an online questionnaire asks for your Social Security and bank account numbers. One problem: While the graphics and pages look authentic, the site is a fake.

Other thieves use more traditional methods of stealing information at tax time, such as dumpster diving and improperly accessing company records. Linda Foley, co-executive director of the Identity Theft Resource Center, understands all too well the danger of tax forms falling into the wrong hands. Her former employer used personal information from her tax forms to open credit cards and a cell phone account in her name.

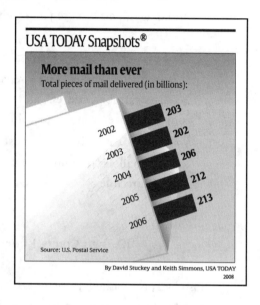

USA TODAY Snapshots®

More mail than ever
Total pieces of mail delivered (in billions):

2002 — 203
2003 — 202
2004 — 206
2005 — 212
2006 — 213

Source: U.S. Postal Service

By David Stuckey and Keith Simmons, USA TODAY
2008

From an identity thief's perspective, tax documents are a goldmine, containing the magic combo of your name and Social Security number, plus bonus information on where you bank.

The following tips can help reduce your risk of tax-related identity theft:

- **Don't believe just anyone who says they're from the IRS.** If you receive a supposed IRS email asking for personal or financial information, delete it or send it to the FTC at spam@uce.gov for investigation. The IRS will never email taxpayers about issues related to their accounts or ask for a Social Security number or financial details over the phone. If in doubt whether a contact from the IRS is authentic, call 800-829-1040.

- **Keep your tax paperwork in a secure location,** such as a locked file cabinet or safe. Shred any paperwork you no longer need before throwing it away.

- **Take protective measures before filing taxes online.** Use updated firewall, antivirus, and antispyware software.

- **Monitor your mail closely during tax season.** Make a list of everyone who pays you, including employers, banks, and brokerages, and be sure you receive copies of what they send to the IRS.

- **Choose your tax professionals as carefully as you would a doctor or lawyer.** Remember, a tax preparer has access to your Social Security number, address, and other private information—and some have been caught misusing them.

- **Mail your tax returns from a post office.** Leaving your tax returns in your mailbox for your postal carrier to pick them up is just inviting trouble.

ID Theft Comes Knocking at Tax Time

Josh had just finished doing his taxes and, in his mind, had already spent the small refund he was expecting from the IRS. You can imagine his excitement when he received a phone call from an "IRS agent," informing him that he was eligible for a $500 rebate for filing his taxes early. All he needed to do was confirm his Social Security number and provide his bank account information for direct deposit of the rebate. (Without direct deposit, he was told, he could not receive the rebate.)

Months later, with no $500 check in sight, Josh's credit report showed that thieves had taken out a new car loan in his name and reactivated a closed credit card account.

What could Josh have done differently? Simply knowing how identity theft scams work could have saved him. The IRS would never have asked him for his personal information over the phone, nor would it require direct deposit for a rebate.

Close Call With a Lottery Scam

After 12 years of teaching high school students, Katie prides herself on her ability to spot scammers. But a recent notification threw her for a loop.

She opened her mail to find a letter saying she'd won a Canadian lottery, along with certified check in her name for $60,000. "I enter a lot of contests and have actually won a few of them," she said. "I didn't remember entering a Canadian lottery, but I figured I must have, if there's a check in the mail."

The check looked legitimate—it had a check number, was issued by a large, reputable bank, and was signed by a company called Citywide Financial Trust of Vancouver. The company advised her that she needed to fax the company's accounting department a form to verify her identity (including a copy of her driver's license and Social Security card) within 24 hours to cash the check.

Fortunately, Katie took the check to her bank before she sent the fax. "They told me that the account had been closed and would bounce," she said. "If they hadn't checked, I would have sent this fraudulent company all my information."

Lottery and Contest Scams

Congratulations! We are pleased to inform you that you're among ten winners of our annual International Automobiles Program. Your name was selected through a computer ballot system drawn from 2,500,000 email addresses of individuals and companies as part of our electronic business promotions program. And you're a lucky winner! Contact us today to receive your portion of the $2,650,000 prize, which will be shared among the winners.

Sounds great, huh? Too bad it's a fraud. In fact, if you ever receive an email or letter congratulating you on winning a lottery or contest you didn't enter, rest assured it's a fraud. Identity thieves around the world increasingly use the telephone and direct mail to convince consumers that they're lucky winners when in reality they're targets of scams. Often, these communications appear to come from legitimate banks or companies. Some might even include counterfeit checks.

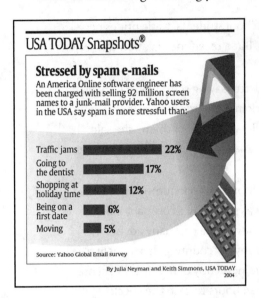

USA TODAY Snapshots®

Stressed by spam e-mails

An America Online software engineer has been charged with selling 92 million screen names to a junk-mail provider. Yahoo users in the USA say spam is more stressful than:

Traffic jams **22%**
Going to the dentist **17%**
Shopping at holiday time **12%**
Being on a first date **6%**
Moving **5%**

Source: Yahoo Global Email survey

By Julia Neyman and Keith Simmons, USA TODAY 2004

When you contact the sender, you'll likely be told that you need to provide proof of your identity or details of your bank accounts or credit cards in order to receive your "winnings." That's all a thief needs to steal your identity.

Fortunately, it's not too hard to spot this type of scam. Any of the following red flags can alert you that something's fishy:

- You're told that you've won a prize, but you didn't enter any contest run by the organization.
- The mail is personally addressed to you but was posted using bulk mail.
- You're asked to provide a bank account or credit card number to cover some type of fee needed to release your winnings.
- You're asked to verify your identity with personal information such as your name, address, date of birth, or Social Security number.
- You're encouraged to reply immediately or the money will be given to someone else.

- An email announcement claims to be from a big company like Publishers Clearing House or Microsoft, but it comes from a free account like Hotmail or Yahoo.

Here are some tips that will help you avoid getting scammed by lottery or contest schemes:

- **Keep your SSN under wraps.** Never provide personal identity information to a company or person you don't know and trust.

- **Know the basic rules of legitimate lotteries.** For example, you can't win a lottery if you haven't entered it. You never have to pay to collect winnings. If you win a lottery, you inform the lottery, not vice versa.

- **Be especially wary of foreign lotteries.** Federal law makes it illegal to play ANY foreign lottery from within the United States. Many other countries have similar laws.

- **Look at who's running the lottery.** Lotteries can be conducted only by government or government-authorized charitable organizations. Lotteries from other organizations are phony.

- **Check that check.** Criminals can create very realistic-looking checks and money orders. If you receive a suspicious-looking check in the mail, bring it to your bank and ask it to investigate the origins.

USA TODAY Snapshots®

Paychecks processed overseas

If your company processed your paycheck overseas to save on costs and remain competitive, how confident are you that your personal data would remain safe and private?

Not confident **87%**

Confident **9%**

Don't know **4%**

Source: 2005 American Payroll Association survey of 29,955 respondents. Margin of error ±1 percentage point.

By Jae Yang and Alejandro Gonzalez, USA TODAY 2006

Blowing the Whistle on Scammers

Now that you've learned how to spot the common scams, you're well equipped to avoid becoming a victim. But don't stop there. By sounding an alarm when you spot one of these scams, you can help prevent victimization of others. Here are a few organizations that investigate scams and help prosecute the criminals behind them:

- **The Better Business Bureau.** Send written complaints to 741 Delaware Avenue, Suite 100, Buffalo, NY 14209-2201, or file complaints online at: www.bbb.org/bbbcomplaints/Welcome.asp.

- **The Federal Trade Commission.** Send written complaints to 6th Street and Pennsylvania Avenue, NW, Room 240, Washington, DC 20580. You can also forward fraudulent emails to spam@ uce.gov.

- **Your state attorney general's office.** You can easily find the number and address online or in the yellow pages.

- **The FBI's Internet Crime Complaint Center.** Report any suspicious activity via a toll-free Corporate Fraud Hotline at 888-622-0117.

- **Financial Crimes Division.** If you've been victimized by one of the foreign money offer schemes, send written documentation to the U.S. Secret Service, Financial Crimes Division, 950 H Street, NW, Washington, DC 20001, or call 202-406-5850.

Be a Savvy Shopper

Have you ever used the Internet to find something you wanted, but gotten worried about online security and headed to a brick and mortar store to actually buy the item? You wouldn't be the first. Many people avoid online shopping because they're worried about identity theft, spyware, and credit card theft.

Cheryl, for example, a formerly loyal online shopper, switched back to regular stores, saying, "I definitely miss the benefits of online shopping. You can't beat the 24-hour convenience and lower prices. But there are so many risks, especially with smaller online shops. You're relying on technology—but can it really protect you?"

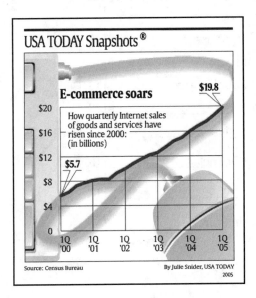

USA TODAY Snapshots®

E-commerce soars

How quarterly Internet sales of goods and services have risen since 2000: (in billions)

Source: Census Bureau

By Julie Snider, USA TODAY 2005

To answer Cheryl's question, online shopping is actually largely secure (yes, it's true). You just need to follow a few precautions and take advantage of the security measures already in place. By contrast, brick-and-mortar stores aren't always as secure from identity thieves as Cheryl and others tend to think. A department store can leak credit card data just as easily as an online store, because it also keeps data on computers that connect to the Internet.

This chapter will help you better understand the risks associated with both online and offline shopping, and provide tips to ensure that your personal and financial information is safe no matter when, where, or how you shop.

How You're Already Protected When Shopping Online

As you can imagine, Internet retailers have a strong interest in making you feel safe buying from them—they depend on your business to stay in business. Various technologies have been developed to reduce your vulnerability to shopping scams, as described below.

The upshot is that, for now at least, you may actually be safer shopping online than offline. More fraud actually occurs in traditional physical channels, such as in-person transactions, than online (as shown by Javelin Strategy & Research, an identity-theft-and-fraud-focused research firm, in its 2007 Identity Fraud Survey Report). When you're using a credit card in your local mall, a store clerk processes the transaction and has access to your private information. When shopping online, your payment details are encrypted, meaning that only the people who authorize your transaction—namely the employees at your bank—see your personal details.

Adults top safety concern?

Identity theft, according to 43% of adults.

Source: Survey by American Express Insurance Services.

Digital certificates

Digital certificates are one of the best ways for online shoppers to tell the legitimate and

USA TODAY Snapshots®

Comfort with online credit card use

Level of agreement to the statement, "I do not feel comfortable giving my credit card number online":

Don't agree or disagree **27%**

Completely agree **22%**

Completely disagree **12%**

Somewhat agree **17%**

Somewhat disagree **22%**

Source: March 2005 online survey 1,390 adults ages 18-54 with Internet access by Frank N. Magid Associates; margin of error ±2.7 percent

By Tracey Wong Briggs and Robert W. Ahrens, USA TODAY 2006

trustworthy sites from the bad ones. Here's how they work. An online merchant applies for a digital certificate from a certification authority, such as Verisign or Thawt, which thoroughly evaluates how the merchant handles online transactions. If approved, the certificate is uploaded to the company's site and a logo is displayed to let customers know they're shopping in a safe place.

If you're shopping on a site that is certified (and you shouldn't shop on any site that isn't), your browser will automatically contact a secured address when you attempt to make a purchase. That address will start with "https" instead of "http." This will trigger the Secure Socket Layer (SSL), which encrypts your sensitive data and scrambles it so that no one can read it while it travels through cyberspace. The only people who can unscramble the code are those with access privileges (namely the people you're sending it to).

USA TODAY Snapshots®

In the online shopping cart
What women purchase online:

Clothing	38%
Books	29%
Household items	11%
Music	9%
Children's items[1]	8%
Electronics	7%

1 – Does not include clothing

Source: The *Consumer Reports* Research Center telephone survey of 427 women for *ShopSmart* magazine. Feb. 22-26. Margin of error, ±4.8 percentage points.

By Mary Cadden and Robert W. Ahrens, USA TODAY
2008

At this point, you'll see a padlock symbol, usually at the bottom of your browser, showing you that your session is secure. The padlocks aren't always foolproof, however, because fraudsters can create similar ones, although it's very difficult to replicate them in a browser. To be on the safe side, click on the padlock image and make sure it displays a valid security certificate. When you check the certificate, the name following "Issued to" should exactly match the site you're visiting. Also be sure to enter the address of any e-commerce site directly into your browser, rather than clicking on a link in an email or other website. These precautions will reduce your chances of falling for a phony website.

Single-use, virtual card numbers

To further protect yourself, you might want to get a single-use credit card for an online purchase. Such cards erase any worries that someone will steal your card number—even if they did, the number wouldn't do them any good. Single-use (or substitute) card numbers are now offered by a number of payment processing companies, including PayPal, CitiBank, and Discover. Check with your current credit card company, which may offer single-use numbers as a benefit with your account.

However, such cards aren't good for every situation. For example, they don't tend to work for hotels or plane tickets, since some merchants require you to show the actual credit card in order to claim your purchase.

Remaining Risks When Shopping Online

Any transactions involving personal and financial information comes with some risk, including that you'll become a victim of identity theft, credit card fraud, or some related scam. Below, we describe when you're most vulnerable.

Risks when using your laptop in a public place

Carole, a 24-year-old blogger from Portland, Maine, loves to work from public places. She often takes her laptop to cafes, parks, libraries, and even pubs, some of which offer free wireless access. While she spends most of her time researching and writing, she occasionally does a little online shopping or banking during breaks. No big deal, right? Wrong!

What Carole doesn't realize is that public hotspots are havens for virtual identity thieves, who can take advantage of unsecured networks to intercept the data flowing between her laptop and the wireless router. Any day now, thieves may get their

USA TODAY Snapshots®

Internet security fears

Fifty-four percent of respondents are more concerned about Internet security now than they were a year ago. Top ways people are reacting:

Installing more security software — 69%

Opting out of special offers — 54%

Buying less online — 41%

Source: TNS NFO and The Conference Board survey of 5,269 respondents. Margin of error ±1 percentage point.

By Darryl Haralson and Robert W. Ahrens, USA TODAY
2005

hands on Carole's passwords and personal information and turn her into a victim of credit card or identity theft. If you're at all like Carole, be sure to read "Play It Safe in Public Hotspots," below.

Play It Safe in Public Hotspots

Few things expose your work to greater security risks than latching onto a public Wi-Fi service.

Computer criminals can "sniff" the traffic in a cafe, or set up a fake hot spot that you might innocently log into. When that happens, watch out: Everything you type goes directly to the host computer, known as an "evil twin." In that scenario, as soon as you get into your online bank account, the evil twin is ready to grab the password.

The best advice for avoiding those situations is to tap only into wireless connections that you trust. Be wary of connections with names such as "free public wifi." Ask at the cafe for the name of its network. Even then, be aware that someone sitting next to you could have set up a network with the same name, such as "Starbucks," that you could tap into unwittingly.

Most security-savvy travelers assume the worst and don't do anything that could cause trouble if it fell into the wrong hands.

"Every packet that goes out over the Internet is observable" by a tech-savvy hacker, says Brett Levine of San Francisco.

Nonetheless, Levine, a vice president at Internet video start-up Dovetail, remains a dedicated cafe worker. He spoke from Hong Kong, at the end of a business trip in which he communicated with "nothing but my laptop. The only connections I've had were in hotel lobbies or cafes. I'm sitting here with my ramen noodles."

He just makes sure that every email he sends is encrypted. And if he's doing anything sensitive online, he makes sure the site is secure.

"If you're on a wireless network, assume it's public," says Alex Stamos, vice president of professional services at iSec Partners, a software security consulting firm in San Francisco and Seattle. "If you're trading stocks, you should be very careful and make sure you're going over the 'https' link."

Play It Safe in Public Hotspots, cont'd

Once you're over "https," you generally are safe, though there are caveats, says Zulfikar Ramzan, a senior principal researcher at Symantec in Cupertino, California. "What 'https' guarantees to you is that whoever is receiving your traffic is receiving it encrypted. But that doesn't guarantee that it goes to the right person."

Take care in small cafes. Dave Zaytsev, a co-owner of Goliath Security in Chicago, warns that the risks are greater in small, local coffee shops than in chains such as Panera Bread, which advertise their secure networks.

"The corporate places are locked down pretty decent," Zaytsev says. "The mom-and-pop places that are just trying to compete, like Joe's Coffee, they don't have consultants. They just go to Best Buy, buy a Linksys router, and have a friend set it up."

Zaytsev has tested some cafes for local television stations' consumer news segments and has often been able to see files stored on individuals' laptops. He's also done "man in the middle" attacks, in which he scans the traffic in a cafe, then steals people's usernames and passwords. (The people in his tests were all willing dupes, he says, usually interns at the TV station.)

 "Watch out for the 'evil twin' when using public Wi-Fi," by Dan Fost, December 12, 2007.

Risks when using a public computer

Public computers, like those in libraries, hotel lobbies, or cafes, can be handy for placing a quick order, particularly when you're traveling. But (as described in Chapter 4), they're far from secure. People may watch you enter your name and other information, or take advantage when you get up for a quick restroom break. Even after you've finished your session, in some cases all the next user has to do is press the "back" button to get right into whatever you were using.

More sophisticated scams also take place. For instance, another user may have installed software (like spyware or key logger software) on the machine, which could steal the credit card numbers you just entered.

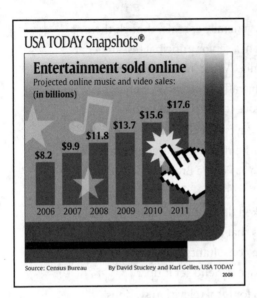

USA TODAY Snapshots®

Entertainment sold online
Projected online music and video sales:
(in billions)

$8.2 $9.9 $11.8 $13.7 $15.6 $17.6

2006 2007 2008 2009 2010 2011

Source: Census Bureau   By David Stuckey and Karl Gelles, USA TODAY 2008

Risks when signing up for "special offers"

Another common type of scam that targets the online shopping crowd is phishing, which you learned about in Chapter 5. While phishing scams run the gamut from fraudsters posing as your credit card company to hackers who want you to download their spyware programs, be especially suspicious of discounted coupons or special offers in your email inbox that appear to come from your favorite online merchants. These may actually redirect you to a phony site that will attempt to steal your credit card information.

Protecting Yourself When Shopping Online

Use the tips below to protect yourself when shopping online. (Also see Chapter 4 for general advice on protecting your online identity and the security of your computer.)

- **Don't shop on your laptop.** Make sure you have a secure connection, and be especially wary of wireless hotspots, such as those in restaurants and coffee shops. Using your neighbor's network is just as risky.

- **Don't shop on a public computer.** Your personal information becomes too easy to grab. If you must use a public computer, clear all cookies and delete temporary Internet files when you're done. (In Firefox, there's a "Tools" option called "Clear private data"; in Explorer, look for the Tools option "Delete Browsing History," and choose "Delete all.") Even better, follow that up by restarting the computer before you leave (if you're allowed to).

- **Shop only on secure websites.** Look at your Internet browser screen. If you see a padlock symbol or see the address bar change from "http" to "https" when you get to the checkout page, you can feel safe completing your purchase. If you don't see these things, shop elsewhere.

- **Shop only with reputable merchants.** If it's your first time shopping with a company, do your homework. Look for certificates from third-party verification companies such as VeriSign or TRUSTe. In addition, a reputable merchant will always list its phone number and contact information. Security concerns aside, how will you return goods or complain if you don't know where to find the company?

Most popular phishing bait used against online shoppers?

eBay and PayPal. These top brands are frequently used by phishers in online identity theft scams (in 63,437 of 300,000 emails analyzed in 2007 by PhishTank). Email with subject lines such as "Your account will be suspended unless you update your account data" are especially common in eBay and PayPal phishing attacks.

- **Watch out for phishing and pharming scams.** No matter what great products or discounts they offer, be very cautious when opening emails and instant messages from unknown sources. For more tips on avoiding these scams (and others), see Chapter 5.

- **If you're teleworking on your laptop, use your company's virtual private network, or VPN.** A VPN is like a secure tunnel through which data gets transferred, encrypted at both ends to keep it safe from prying eyes.

What's Gender Got to Do With It?

Men, it appears, are more comfortable shopping online than women—and spend more freely. This was shown in a 2008 survey by Javelin Strategy and Research, which also revealed that:

- 91% of the people surveyed planned to make a purchase online in the next three months.
- While 16% of men planned to spend between $500 and $1,000 in the next three months, only 10% of women planned to do the same.
- When buying products online or in person, 68% of men as compared to 57% of women said they're as comfortable either way.
- The majority of women, or 62%, but only just over half the men, or 53%, say they'd buy more online if they felt better protected against identity theft.

Risks When Shopping in Stores

Consider this scenario: You're paying for merchandise in a trendy boutique, and strike up a conversation with Leia, the friendly sales clerk. She compliments you on your purse or tie, and you tell her it was a birthday gift. She says, "Oh! When was your birthday?"

You've just innocently given Leia one of the last pieces of information she needs to steal your identity. Through the store database, she can already access your name, address, phone number, and more. Now she can trick companies or government agencies into giving her any additional details she needs to complete the picture. (Neutral topics like the weather and sports are starting to look pretty good again, yes?)

Now, imagine you stop by the bagel shop on your way to work, and while paying with your debit card, Chuck, a chipper clerk, entertains you with stories about his "crazy" morning. You're so distracted that you don't notice he swipes your card through two devices, and watches your fingers closely as you enter your PIN. Now he has your card data and PIN, which he can use to empty your bank account. Or even if Chuck is a good guy, other, less-honest customers may memorize your PIN or even take pictures of your card using a cell phone camera and follow you outside to steal your card.

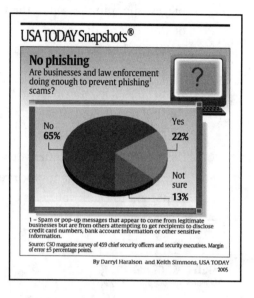

USA TODAY Snapshots®

No phishing
Are businesses and law enforcement doing enough to prevent phishing[1] scams?

No **65%**

Yes **22%**

Not sure **13%**

1 – Spam or pop-up messages that appear to come from legitimate businesses but are from others attempting to get recipients to disclose credit card numbers, bank account information or other sensitive information.

Source: CSO magazine survey of 459 chief security officers and security executives. Margin of error ±5 percentage points.

By Darryl Haralson and Keith Simmons, USA TODAY 2005

Another problem (a harder one to control) is that most stores keep your name and other information in a database, so you're relying on their ability to keep that data secure. Customers who shopped in the physical stores of discount retailers TJ Maxx and Marshalls learned this lesson the hard way. Millions who paid via credit or debit cards in physical locations received alerts in 2006 that their personal information had been intercepted and stolen. Hackers reportedly broke into the stores' central databases and accessed millions of financial transactions.

Protecting Yourself When Shopping in Stores

When you're out shopping, your wallet, other people, and various card-swiping machines may all come together in ways they usually don't. So although you've heard some of these tips from us before, let's go over the most important ways to guard your personal information:

- **Watch for people watching you.** Be aware of people standing nearby or taking pictures when you're at the checkout counter.

- **Avoid ordinary theft.** Shopping malls are often crowded, so pay close attention to your wallet or purse, lest they be pickpocketed or stolen. Bring only the cards you need, and leave your Social Security card and checkbook at home.

- **Be extra careful during the holiday season.** Identity thieves, con artists, and grinches of all sorts are out in full force during the biggest shopping season of the year, waiting to take advantage of stressed and distracted shoppers. Carry your purse or wallet closely and be aware of people around you, especially at the sales counter.

- **Write "Check my photo ID" in permanent ink on your credit card.** Adding this request near your signature tells cashiers to make sure it's really you before processing your card.

- **Later, check your bills.** After you've gone on a mega shopping spree, you may not want to see your credit card statements. But it's important to check your bills carefully for unfamiliar purchases. Keep your shopping receipts in one place so you can easily validate that your billing statement is accurate. (Even without identity theft, mistakes happen.)

You can never be too safe when it comes to your personal information. By understanding the risks and taking extra precautions, you can shop until you drop—online or offline—while enjoying peace of mind that your identity is safe.

USA TODAY Snapshots®

High cost of learning

Total back-to-college spending in 2007: (in billions)

Textbooks — $15.6

Electronics or computer-related equipment — $12.8

Dorm or apartment furnishings — $5.4

School supplies — $3.1

Shoes — $3.0

Source: National Retail Federation

By David Stuckey and Karl Gelles, USA TODAY 2007

Take Control of Your Data

Every day, data is collected from each of us, usually without our knowledge and sometimes even without our consent. Think about a typical day in your life. You pay your bills and buy things with your credit cards and checks, leaving a data trail that shows what you bought, when you bought it, how much you paid, and (if you're shopping online), what other stuff you looked at. You swipe your supermarket loyalty card when buying groceries, contributing to a massive database that tracks what you bought and when. You drive your car through an electronic tollbooth, where your account is debited and your trips are tracked. At home or work, you surf the Web, make online purchases, and IM your best friend. Every action you take adds to your growing trail of mouse clicks and other data.

"In my entire career, I have never encountered a crime as easy to pull off as identity theft. The main reason is that so much personal information is widely and publicly available, there for anyone to take."
Frank Abagnale, author of Catch Me If You Can

And it doesn't stop there. At times, you might also subscribe to a new magazine, sign up for a music club, fill out a warranty card, donate money to a charity, register to vote, buy a hot stock, make a telephone call, or visit your dentist. All of these transactions leave a data trail.

No matter who collects information about you or where it's stored, you can count on one thing—data aggregators will find it. These aggregators (also known as data brokers, data miners, and data merchants), make billions by collecting every morsel of personal, professional, financial, and medical information they can dig up about people, and then selling it for profit—probably multiple times.

For the most part, data aggregation isn't harmful. In fact, it helps companies provide better goods and services to consumers, and helps employers, insurers, and lenders make better decisions faster. This results in the conveniences we've come to rely on, such as instant loans, quick insurance quotes, and targeted coupons and advertisements.

However, there's a dark side to having your personal information so easily accessible, as we'll describe in this chapter. We'll also show you how simple awareness and a few precautions will help you can enjoy the convenience of modern technologies without compromising your identity.

Behind the Scenes: How Your Data Gets Collected

Even before the age of computers, businesses began keeping detailed records of their customers, for reasons ranging from recommending other products to chasing after an unreturned video. Schools have long kept records of their students and alumni, government agencies have maintained records of people they've served, and doctors have kept notes on illnesses and medications. The difference now is that they're all putting this information onto computers or online databases.

Added to that, the Internet has introduced the ability to track your movements, quite apart from the basic data you enter. Everywhere we go, we're tracked by Internet cookies. Online companies such as Google, Microsoft, and Yahoo take note of what products, entertainment, and music people like and what they search for, so that they can boost their online advertising revenue.

Enter the aggregators, who have fashioned themselves as central collection points for all this information. There are thousands of them, large and small, currently operating in the United States. Before today, you may not have heard the names Acxiom and LexisNexis, but you can bet they'd heard of you. In fact, they and other

USA TODAY Snapshots®

Internet use up for young and old
Growth continues in the percentages of youths and adults using the Internet:

■ 2000
■ 2004

Youths 12-17: 73% (2000), 87% (2004)
Adults: 56% (2000), 66% (2004)

Source: Pew Internet & American Life Project

By Marcy E. Mullins, USA TODAY
2005

aggregators (including the credit bureaus) probably have pages-long files of your personal information. And this is despite the fact that you've probably never directly given them permission to gather this data in the first place. How exactly do they get it?

Much of the information gathered and sold by data brokers comes from public records—courthouses, county tax assessors, and Department of Motor Vehicle databases—many of which have inadequate restrictions on how the information is secured. For example, a 2008 audit showed that Colorado's Division of Motor Vehicles regularly sends personal information over the Internet without encryption and inadequately limits access to its databases. Even Social Security numbers can be readily accessed from some public records.

USA TODAY Snapshots®

Specialists in spam
The USA tops the list of the 10 countries that produce the most junk e-mail, or "spam." Known spammers as of Jan. 15:

USA	2,071
China	371
Russia	252
Japan	200
South Korea	165
Canada	151
United Kingdom	143
Hong Kong	143
Germany	127
Taiwan	125

Source: The Spamhaus Project

By Melanie Eversley and Robert W. Ahrens, USA TODAY 2007

Data aggregators are also willing to pay for personal information (some of which you might have thought was private). That's how they get pieces of data like unpublished phone and cell numbers, phone records, and customer lists from companies like Capital One and Hilton Hotels.

Although you may think you're being careful about who you give your personal information to, handing a tidbit of data to one business or person may quickly put it into the hands of others. Consider your email inbox. If you're bombarded by spam, it could partly be because you gave your email address to a Web-based company. When you give out your telephone number or address, the same thing happens. You may think your cell phone is officially unlisted, but if you've ever used it to order a pizza, the pizza delivery company may have sold it.

While most data aggregation companies play by the rules in gathering information, some data resellers have been caught breaking them. It's not uncommon for these companies to use private investigators to dig up personal facts, who sometimes tell outright lies in order to obtain confidential information.

Data for Sale—All Kinds

There are three main categories of information that data brokers mine and sell: public records, publicly available information, and nonpublic information.

Public record information

Public information includes everything collected by a government body and accessible by the public, such as birth certificates, voter registrations, bankruptcy filings, and tax lien records. While anyone can get ahold of these, doing so can be expensive and time-consuming. Data brokers can quickly and inexpensively collect and organize this information in bulk, providing a one-stop shop for their customers.

Publicly available information

Data brokers also offer information from readily available sources such as phone books, newspapers, and Internet sites.

Nonpublic information

This is where data aggregation gets controversial. Data brokers have the means to obtain personal information that's not generally available to the public, including information:

- people give to businesses when buying products or services (name, address, date of birth, marital status, email address, credit card numbers, and even Social Security number, for example)
- about consumer transactions, such as the types of products someone buys, travel itineraries, or insurance claims
- from applications submitted to obtain credit, employment, insurance, or other services, and
- from applications or signups for contests, warranties, email accounts, photo-sharing companies, social networking sites, and more.

Who They Sell Your Data To

The snapshot that data aggregators create of you—or pieces of that snapshot—will be sold countless times in your lifetime. Most of the aggregators' customers are legitimate: Banks and landlords buy information to ensure that their applicants are creditworthy. The police use it to track down criminals and terrorists. Marketers use customer data to help develop products and promotions appealing to specific customer segments.

Sometimes, data aggregators actually sell government and business organizations the very same information collected from them in the first place. With government agencies notoriously inefficient at sharing information, the U.S. government spent an estimated $30 million in 2005 buying personal data in order to locate witnesses, track terrorist groups, conduct research, and locate people for various reasons, including collecting child support, settling outstanding debts, or warning people they'd been exposed to certain viruses.

USA TODAY Snapshots®

Searching for jobs online
How many hours a day do you spend searching for jobs online?

Less than one hour **42%**
One to three hours **47%**
Three to seven hours **8%**
More than seven hours **2%**

Note: Total doesn't add up to 100 due to rounding

Source: RiseSmart survey of 1,000 job-seekers. Margin of error ±2 percentage points.

By Jae Yang and Alejandro Gonzalez, USA TODAY 2008

Of course, the aggregators' customers also include criminals planning to commit identity theft. The media contains many stories about how someone's personal information was lost, stolen, or otherwise compromised due to misuses of aggregated personal information—like in May 2007, when *The New York Times* reported that consumer data broker InfoUSA made huge profits selling lists of senior citizens and other easy targets to possible identity thieves and con artists. Particularly damning was that, according to the article, one of InfoUSA's lists of names proclaimed: "These people are gullible. They want to believe that their luck can change."

As that example shows, the identity thief may not start out targeting you personally. Data aggregators can supply lists of potential victims. For example, a list of 601 charity donors in Pleasanton, California, can be purchased from USAData for $75. A list of 36,000 people who earn more than $150,000 per year in New York City, including names and phone numbers, runs a mere $1,800.

Most aggregators don't intentionally sell to thieves, but nor do they make it terribly difficult for thieves to pose as legitimate customers. To deal with the problem, the larger data aggregation companies have embarked on a policy of not selling consumer information to individuals, and being increasingly careful about whom they provide certain types of information to.

However, there are plenty of smaller data resellers out there who don't follow such policies. For example, many private investigation companies use data aggregators to get the "dirt" on people they're hired to investigate. Specialized data aggregators such as ExcellentDetective.com sell unlisted phone numbers, birth dates, attorney records, DUI files, and much more. Their online advertisement might be tempting to more people than honest detectives: "Just think of all the dirt & secrets you could get on your friends, family, coworkers, and even your neighbors with Excellent Detective by joining right now."

Other companies like Abika.com offer to identify the physical address, including street name, behind an email or instant message. Gum-shoes.com promises that "if the information is out there, our licensed investigators can find it."

No One Is Immune

To test the availability of consumer information, U.S. Senator Ted Stevens instructed his staff to steal his identity. He was not pleased with the results. They came back with a history of his online activities, as well as information on his daughter's rental property. For a small fee, they could have bought his Social Security number.

The upshot is that, for just a few dollars, an identity thief can piece together enough information to steal your identity. Your address might cost a quarter. Got an unpublished phone number? That'll cost about $20. Your Social Security number might go for $10. And $50 would buy a complete background check, including your date of birth, phone number, address, employer, property records, and perhaps even a list of your roommates and relatives.

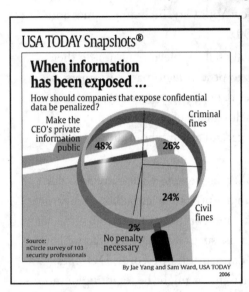

USA TODAY Snapshots®

When information has been exposed ...

How should companies that expose confidential data be penalized?

Make the CEO's private information public **48%**

Criminal fines **26%**

24%

Civil fines

2% No penalty necessary

Source: nCircle survey of 103 security professionals

By Jae Yang and Sam Ward, USA TODAY 2006

What's more, identity thieves can buy far more than your basic data. The aggregators can tell them what your mortgage payments are, where you shop, how much money you owe on your car loan, what bank you use, whether you subscribe to *Good Housekeeping* or *Playboy*, and whether you're more likely to visit Las Vegas or Dubai. Armed with all this information, a criminal could conduct a highly targeted identity theft scam against you personally, such as phishing or pretexting.

For example, if a phisher learns that you owe $2,000 on your Honda Civic, you might receive an email that looks just like the ones you get from your lender and includes language like: "Click here to lower your Honda Civic payments from $2,000 to $1,000." Because the message includes accurate details about your loan, you're more likely to be duped.

Are there any restrictions on who can look at your data? Yes, although they cover only credit records, and even these restrictions aren't always upheld. The Federal Fair Credit Reporting Act requires that your credit record be provided only to those with legitimate business purposes, including lenders, landlords, employers, insurance providers, and government and law enforcement agencies. Of these, only employers are legally required to get your written permission, although most potential creditors, insurers, and landlords pull your report only after you've submitted an application. Still, it's well known in the data aggregation industry that many data resellers simply rely on their customers' word that they have a legitimate business need.

Also, the CRAs create massive files of personal information about you, which they package as credit reports, consumer reports, and marketing lists and sell to lenders, merchants, landlords, and other businesses. Once the information is out of your credit file and in the hands of private businesses, there is little regulation of how it can be used or shared.

Can Someone Really Buy Your Social Security Number?

Perhaps the biggest concern for consumers is that Social Security numbers, the key ingredients for identity theft, can be purchased through data aggregators. Many schools, insurance companies, and doctors' offices still use the Social Security number as your account number, and then share your records with data aggregators. It doesn't take a genius to figure out what your nine-digit account number represents. And data aggregators themselves—particularly credit reporting agencies—use your SSN to help link pieces of your consumer file together, like your driver's license record, credit card account activity, and employment history.

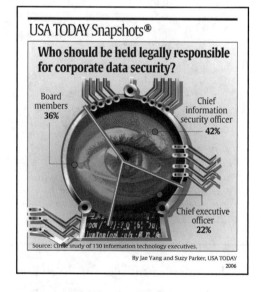

USA TODAY Snapshots®

Who should be held legally responsible for corporate data security?

Board members
36%

Chief information security officer
42%

Chief executive officer
22%

Source: Circle study of 130 information technology executives.

By Jae Yang and Suzy Parker, USA TODAY 2006

To make matters worse, SSNs are sometimes made publicly available due to the lax security practices of private and government organizations. For three years, the California Secretary of State's office routinely placed thousands of documents containing Social Security numbers on the Internet and then sold them to the public for $6 each. (When the security breach was discovered in 2006, officials shut the site down immediately.) In addition, many local government agencies have been known to write Social Security numbers on tax liens and other public records.

No law prohibits Social Security numbers from being bought and sold, so it's unlikely that ChoicePoint and other data aggregators will stop selling them anytime soon. For this reason, you should treat your SSN like it's your bank account PIN. Unless it's absolutely necessary and requested by a legitimate organization for a legitimate reason (we'll dive deeper into this later in this chapter), always refuse to give it out.

Will Data Protections Improve Anytime Soon?

Existing laws and rules on how information can be bought and sold are ill-suited to protecting consumers. Because many identity theft cases and data breaches have been linked to privacy flaws in the data aggregation industry, major data aggregators, such as LexisNexis and Experian, have promised to restrict the availability of such data.

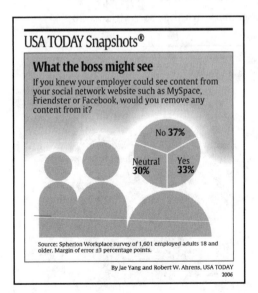

USA TODAY Snapshots®

What the boss might see

If you knew your employer could see content from your social network website such as MySpace, Friendster or Facebook, would you remove any content from it?

No **37%**

Neutral **30%**   Yes **33%**

Source: Spherion Workplace survey of 1,601 employed adults 18 and older. Margin of error ±3 percentage points.

By Jae Yang and Robert W. Ahrens, USA TODAY
2006

This is good news. As a result of reforms by the major data aggregators, the majority of the data is now collected for legitimate purposes: for employment screening, insurance underwriting, credit checks, debt collection, and law enforcement agencies. In addition, most reputable data aggregators restrict who can gain access to sensitive data like Social Security numbers. And most companies claim to thoroughly screen their customers before releasing your data to them.

ID Theft Guardian Angels?

For a few hours a day, Steven Peisner calls strangers across the U.S.A.—sometimes at night—and reads to them their Social Security numbers and credit card data.

Though many recipients immediately suspect he is an ID thief, Peisner's intent is just the opposite: He is a digital whistle-blower.

"My motivation is to be a good citizen and put a dent in (fraudulent email) phishing scams," says Peisner, president of SellitSafe.com, which provides antiphishing services for online merchants. He works closely with law enforcement and computer-security experts. Peisner, 43, is one of several avenging angels nationwide looking out for the well-being of ID-theft victims. They share a fervent desire to publicize the widespread availability of stolen personal data on the Internet.

- Betty "BJ" Ostergren, a former insurance-claims supervisor in Virginia, occasionally warns consumers that their Social Security numbers are posted on public government websites. For the past four years, she has spent several hours a day digging through sites for Social Security numbers. So far, she's uncovered 18,000 records.

- Janice Forster, 50, a paralegal in North Carolina, started FindMyId.com, a website devoted to educating consumers about ID theft. She mailed more than 100 letters to North Carolina residents informing them that their personal information is available on the Internet.

"I just want to make a difference," says Forster, who had never before been involved in a grassroots movement. "In good conscience, I can't watch this happen to people."

That's why Peisner called Christopher Buckley, a high school teacher in Los Angeles, late at night during Labor Day weekend to inform Buckley that his credit card number was on the ccpower forum, a black-market website where criminals deal in stolen

ID Theft Guardian Angels?, cont'd

personal data. "I was shocked he called but glad he did," says Buckley, 31, who mistakenly forked over information via email to someone claiming to be from PayPal.

There is a method to Peisner's madness. As phishing continues to escalate, the safest course for consumers may be to warn them over the phone. There is little in the way of software to warn consumers they have been phished.

"We need to take control of the situation," says Peisner, who does not profit from his advice to consumers but sells his company's services to businesses. "The police have their hands full with these types of cases. It's up to consumers like me to take action."

 "Good cybercitizens keep watch over ID-theft victims," by Jon Swartz, September 28, 2006.

However, as various breaches and investigations have shown, plenty of holes remain in the data aggregation system, raising questions about the tradeoffs we accept when we fill out a form or sign up for a free service.

Are You Giving Out More Data Than You Need To?

When it comes to leaks of your data, you may have to share the guilt. Many consumers say that privacy is important to them, but then hand over vital personal information as soon as someone asks for it.

Google's Gmail service is a good example. In 2004, when Gmail launched, many people laughed. Who would sign up for an email service that would scan your emails and send you ads based on what those emails said? Surely they'd be too concerned about potential privacy. The scoffers were wrong. Today, Gmail is booming with millions of happy, privacy-free users. (And, to be fair, Gmail is fairly safe; while Google shares your surfing habits with other companies and organizations, it doesn't sell personally identifiable information.)

Whenever you sign up with a company for a service that requires a password (such as Gmail, My Yahoo, or a personalized search), you're handing over the keys to your online identity. For example, if you sign up for Google's Desktop Search, you'll be able to quickly and easily search files stored on your computer—and so will Google, and anyone who manages to breach its security.

USA TODAY Snapshots®

Most think employers protect personal information

Are you confident that your employer adequately protects your vital personal information from data/identity theft, including the amount of your salary, Social Security number, etc.?

Yes 85%

No 14%

Don't know 2%

Note: Total doesn't add up to 100 due to rounding
Source: American Payroll Association survey of 33,128 workers.
Margin of error ±1 percentage point.

By Jae Yang and Keith Simmons, USA TODAY
2006

Many consumers behave in ways that seem to directly contradict their demands for privacy online. They post private information, photos, and personal files on public websites, especially social networking sites. Identity thieves can use these to create "identity packets," which help them conduct pretexting and phishing scams.

But even for the careful consumers, it's hard to avoid the conclusion that data brokers, corporations, and the government know more about you than you think—or would like. So what should you do? Everything in your power to take control of your data!

Taking Control of Your Data

A legislative solution reining in the data aggregators may be far down the road, so how can you protect yourself in the meantime? The short answer is to be careful and guarded with your information, and take action to protect it any time you feel it may be at risk.

Can You Trust Corporate America?

When customers sign up for a free Hotmail email account from Microsoft, they're required to submit their name, age, gender, and ZIP code. But that's not all the software giant knows about them.

Microsoft takes notice of what time of day they access their inboxes. And it goes to the trouble of finding out how much money folks in their neighborhood earn.

Why? It knows a florist will pay a premium to have a coupon for roses reach males 30–40, earning good wages, who check their email during lunch hour on Valentine's Day.

Microsoft is one of many companies collecting and aggregating data in new ways so sophisticated that many customers may not even realize they're being watched. Brick-and-mortar stores, afraid of being left behind, are ramping up data collection and processing efforts, too, says JupiterResearch analyst Patti Freeman Evans.

The result: Corporate America is creating increasingly detailed portraits of each consumer, whether they're aware of it or not.

Companies say they can be trusted to do so responsibly. Yahoo, for instance, has a strict ban on selling data from its customer registration lists. And Microsoft says it won't purchase an individual's income history—just the average income from his or her ZIP code.

Some consumers aren't reassured. Privacy advocates are worried, too. "Think about it: A handful of powerful entities know a tremendous amount of information about you," says Jeff Chester, executive director of the Center for Digital Democracy. "Today they manipulate you into what kind of soap to buy, tomorrow it might be who you should pray for or who you should vote for."

"Data miners dig a little deeper," by Michelle Kessler and Byron Acohido, July 11, 2006.

By now, you know that you're allowed a free credit report from the three major credit reporting bureaus once a year. (If you forgot how to order it, go back to Chapter 3.) That's one good way to check for identity theft, no matter where the thief got the information about you.

Here are the best ways to limit the amount of information circulating about you:

- **Opt out of marketing lists.** The big-three credit bureaus (Equifax, TransUnion, and Experian) make a pretty penny selling your information to credit card companies, who then send you preapproved applications. To remove your name from their marketing lists, simply call their opt-out line: 888-567-8688, or visit www.optoutprescreen.com. You can choose to remove your name permanently or for a two-year period.

- **Provide your Social Security number only when absolutely necessary.** It may seem like everyone asks you for your Social Security number. Just say no, unless there's no other option. For example, when filling out tax forms, applying for a job, or opening a financial account, you'll need to provide it. But if a school, medical office, marketer, or business asks you for the number, always ask why it's required, how it will be used, what will happen if you don't provide it, and whether you can create an alternate number to identify your file or account.

- **Sign up for the Direct Marketing Association's (DMA) Mail Preference Service.** The DMA manages a Mail Preference Service that allows you to opt out of receiving direct mail marketing from participating companies for five years. When you sign up, your name is added to a "delete" list and sent to direct mail marketers. To register, send a letter to: Direct Marketing Association, Mail Preference Service, P.O. Box 643, Carmel, NY, 10512; or register online at www.the-dma.org/consumers/offmailinglist. html. (Unfortunately, registering also means you'll stop receiving catalogs from places you like.)

- **Opt out of telemarketing.** Enroll in the Federal Trade Commission's Do Not Call registry by visiting www.donotcall.gov or calling 888-382-1222. This prevents companies from selling your information to at least some others.

- **Review privacy policies whenever you visit websites.** Your favorite online surfing spots can collect a lot of information about your visit—what model of computer you use, what other sites you've visited, what searches you conducted, and much more. Sites that ask you to provide even a small amount of personal information can combine bits and pieces of information about you over time to create a snapshot of your online habits. Before providing any information, wade through the site's privacy policy to find out how the company collects, shares, and protects your personal information, then decide whether it's worth the exchange.

- **Don't fill out surveys on warranty cards.** Simply provide your name, address, and necessary product information—you're not required to complete the surveys. Be especially careful with direct mail surveys from companies you don't know or trust.

- **Don't give out sensitive information.** This means on the phone, through the mail, or over the Internet, unless you've initiated the contact or you're sure that it's from a company or organization you trust. When in doubt, contact the company to verify its legitimacy. Even then, provide only the information you know they need to know.

If you wish, you can also find out what sort of consumer data is being compiled on you, including about your employment, rental, and medical history. The list below includes the companies most likely to have the scoop on your habits and history. While not all of these organizations will have records on you, you'll likely be on file at many of them. For a small fee, you can order your consumer files. If you find major errors, you may want to dispute them. (It may not make a huge difference to your chances of becoming an identity theft victim; but if, for instance, you're applying for a Catholic school teaching job, you don't want your background check erroneously reporting that you've worked at a strip club for the past five years.)

Companies That Compile Consumer Information	
Insurance Records	
ChoiceTrust—CLUE Report	866-312-8076
ISO Insurance Services	800-627-3487
Medical Information Bureau	866-692-6901
Employment Records	
ChoicePoint	866-312-8075
Acxiom	800-853-3228
Check-Writing Records	
ChexSystems	800-428-9623
TeleCheck	800-835-3243
Tenant Records	
ChoicePoint Tenant History	877-448-5732

Defending Yourself Against Data Breaches

Despite your best efforts, you might read in the paper—or get an actual letter informing you—that a database containing your name has been breached. Through no fault of your own, such breaches can deliver personal information such as your name, Social Security number, driver's license number, bank or credit account numbers, Personal Identification Numbers (PIN), passwords, or medical information, into the hands of identity thieves.

Approximately 49 million American adults have been informed over the last three years that their personal information had been lost, stolen, or improperly disclosed. (Source: Survey by Harris Interactive.) The majority of these notifications came from government agencies and financial institutions. For example:

Data Dumps: What to Toss

Has your file cabinet become a chaotic pile of clutter? If so, it's time to dust off your shredder and dump some of that data. Here's a guide on what to keep and what to toss.

What to shred every month

- Credit card, ATM, and bank deposit receipts; these can be tossed after you've checked them against your monthly bank statement, unless you'll file them as deductible expenses when you do your taxes.
- Sales receipts for minor purchases, as long as you're sure you won't want to return the items.

What to shred every year

- Monthly bank and credit card statements.
- Monthly or quarterly brokerage and mutual fund statements, after you've checked them against your yearly statement.
- Monthly mortgage statements, after you've checked them against your yearly statement.
- Phone and utility bills.
- Paycheck stubs, after you've checked them against your annual W-2 or 1099 forms.

What to keep for seven years

- W-2 and 1099 forms.
- Annual statements from credit card companies.
- Canceled checks and sales receipts for tax-deductible expenses, including medical bills, deductible business expenses, and annual mortgage interest statements.

What to keep indefinitely

- Annual tax returns. The IRS has three years after a return is filed to audit a return; six years if a taxpayer omits more than 25% of gross income from his or her return; and an unlimited time if fraud is discovered.

Data Dumps: What to Toss, cont'd

- Annual statements from financial services companies (401(k) statements, mutual fund statements, bank records, and the like).
- Insurance, housing, and investment property purchase records. As long as they're active, and for six years after a property is sold, retain insurance policies, leases, titles, mortgage loan papers, property bills of purchase, and receipts for home improvements.

- A U.S. Transportation Security Administration vendor reported that a laptop containing unencrypted personal records of 33,000 customers seeking to enroll in the company's Registered Traveler program was stolen in August 2008.

- A laptop containing the names, birthdays, and Social Security numbers of more than 26 million military veterans was stolen from the home of an employee at the Department of Veterans Affairs (VA) in 2006.

- A data intrusion into the Hannaford supermarket chain's network in March 2008 exposed nearly 4.2 million credit and debit cards and led to 1,800 reported cases of fraud.

- Harvard University notified 10,000 applicants in March of 2008 that their Social Security numbers and other personal data may have been accessed by hackers through a file-sharing site.

- The Department of Justice indicted 11 people in 2008 for hacking into the databases of several major U.S. retailers—OfficeMax, Boston Market, Barnes & Noble, Sports Authority, Forever 21, Marshalls, and TJ Maxx. More than 40 million credit and debit card numbers were stolen.

Fortunately, not all data breaches result in identity theft. But if you find out that a breach has occured, it's in your interest to take precautions. Here's how:

- **Take notifications seriously.** Thanks to state laws and company policies, many organizations notify victims after a data breach has occurred. Be sure to read this correspondence and take advantage of any assistance (such as free credit monitoring) they might offer. If you have questions, call the organization's customer service line.

- **Freeze your credit as soon as you hear about the breach.** A credit freeze blocks access to your credit file unless you authorize the credit bureaus to release your report. This dramatically reduces your chances of becoming a victim. ●

Clamp Down on Thefts of Your Health Coverage

While ordinary identity theft can wreak havoc on your credit record and bank accounts, something called medical identity theft can hurt in other ways. A thief might use your personal information to obtain insurance money, prescription drugs, or medical services. As a result, you could get stuck with medical bills that aren't yours, and your medical chart may be tainted by the thief's information (such as blood type or history of illness). In the case of a medical emergency, the results could be life-threatening. Or you could become uninsurable or unemployable because your files show medical problems or procedures you've never actually had.

To combat this threat, this chapter will teach you:

- what medical identity theft is

- how it can happen to you

- how to prevent it, and

- what to do if you become a victim.

At least 250,000 to 500,000 Americans have already been victimized by medical identity theft. But privacy experts believe many more victims are out there, as this crime is underreported and difficult to detect. Kevin Lee, Founder and Principal of STAT Revenue Consulting, which assists hospitals with revenue and insurance payment recovery, confirms: "In reviewing a hospital's financial records, my team has seen an increase in the occurrences of medical identity theft. And when expensive services are involved—for example, a cardiac defibrillator implant or laparoscopic cholecystectomy, the charges can run into the hundreds of thousands of dollars."

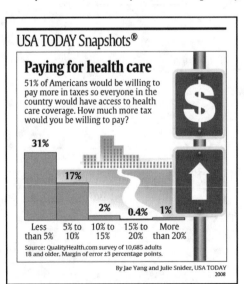

USA TODAY Snapshots®

Paying for health care

51% of Americans would be willing to pay more in taxes so everyone in the country would have access to health care coverage. How much more tax would you be willing to pay?

31%
17%
2%   0.4%   1%

Less than 5% | 5% to 10% | 10% to 15% | 15% to 20% | More than 20%

Source: QualityHealth.com survey of 10,685 adults 18 and older. Margin of error ±3 percentage points.

By Jae Yang and Julie Snider, USA TODAY 2008

Theft of Your Access to Medical Care

Consider the following scenario: You're rushed to the hospital with a severe case of appendicitis. After looking at your chart, the doctors note that your appendix was removed last year. But your appendix wasn't removed—an identity thief used your information to have the surgery that you now need. And, assuming you're conscious, you've now got an argument on your hands to convince doctors that there's an important reason you miraculously have no surgical scar!

Similarly, if an identity thief checks into the hospital using your name, and is tested for blood type, the result will be recorded in your medical history. If you're ever in a serious accident or urgently need blood, you'd better hope that the doctors double check what they read on your chart.

The sad truth is that many medical identity thieves aren't trying to make money—they need health services or medications for which they can't pay or aren't covered. An estimated 47 million Americans currently lack health insurance.

For example, an elderly woman was arrested for using another woman's identity to charge Medicaid for thousands of dollars in medical services and prescription drugs. She was busted when the billing department noticed duplicate charges—apparently, the victim had many of the same health problems as the thief. In another case, a Philadelphia man used another man's name and health insurance information to obtain tens of thousands of dollars in medical care at five different hospitals. Neither criminal received cash from their scam—they just needed medical attention.

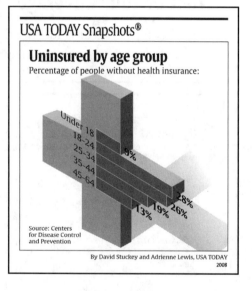

USA TODAY Snapshots®

Uninsured by age group

Percentage of people without health insurance:

Under 18
18-24
25-34
35-44
45-64

9%
8%
13% 19% 26%

Source: Centers for Disease Control and Prevention

By David Stuckey and Adrienne Lewis, USA TODAY
2008

No Social Security Number Needed

To use your medical benefits, an identity thief needs only your name, address, and insurance policy number—not your Social Security number. An identity thief could walk into a medical office with just your name and medical insurance number and receive services— unless, of course, the doctor knows you personally.

Theft of Your Coverage Dollars

In another type of medical identity theft, the criminals—often members of organized crime rings and assisted by health care insiders (including doctors and nurses)—steal patient information and sell it on the black market.

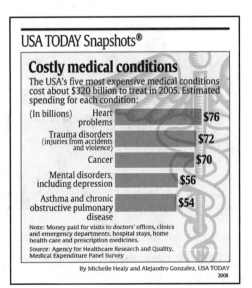

USA TODAY Snapshots®

Costly medical conditions

The USA's five most expensive medical conditions cost about $320 billion to treat in 2005. Estimated spending for each condition:

(In billions)

Heart problems — $76

Trauma disorders (injuries from accidents and violence) — $72

Cancer — $70

Mental disorders, including depression — $56

Asthma and chronic obstructive pulmonary disease — $54

Note: Money paid for visits to doctors' offices, clinics and emergency departments, hospital stays, home health care and prescription medicines.

Source: Agency for Healthcare Research and Quality, Medical Expenditure Panel Survey

By Michelle Healy and Alejandro Gonzalez, USA TODAY 2008

These thieves aren't looking to get health care. They're in it for the money. They steal patients' medical records and doctors' billing codes, which they use to submit bogus bills to insurers. Victims may be stuck paying medical bills for services they never used.

For example, one medical office worker stole over 1,000 patient records and sold them to an identity theft ring for $10 per file. In another case, a psychiatrist used stolen patient information to create medical files that included false diagnoses of drug addiction, depression, and other medical problems. He then submitted these files to insurance companies, billing them for services he never provided. The insurance companies were hit with the charges, but the patients had a problem of their own—false information now tainted their files.

Law enforcement officials have also reported a new and disturbing trend related to medical identity theft, in which organized criminal groups set up seemingly legitimate medical clinics and lure patients in under the guise of providing free health screening or services. Once they con their "patients" into handing over insurance information, they pair this data with stolen physician billing codes and send bogus bills to insurance companies. By the time the insurance companies catch on, the thieves are long gone. One gang of thieves set up a clinic that raked in nearly a million dollars in just three months.

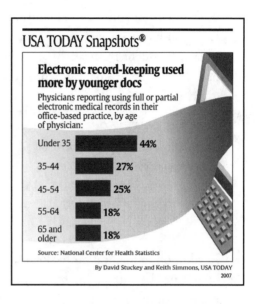

USA TODAY Snapshots®

Electronic record-keeping used more by younger docs

Physicians reporting using full or partial electronic medical records in their office-based practice, by age of physician:

Age	Percentage
Under 35	44%
35-44	27%
45-54	25%
55-64	18%
65 and older	18%

Source: National Center for Health Statistics

By David Stuckey and Keith Simmons, USA TODAY 2007

How Electronic Record Keeping Makes You Vulnerable

Once upon a time, people maintained close relationships with their family doctors, whom they trusted to keep their information private. Their medical histories were stored mainly on paper files, locked away in dusty cabinets. Most people didn't worry about their files being stolen or shared.

Fast forward to the present day. Most medical offices and hospitals have embraced electronic health records (EHRs), which allow full medical files to be easily and inexpensively shared. For example, if your family doctor is in New Jersey and you're having surgery in Philadelphia, your doctor can—within seconds—electronically transfer your complete medical history to your surgeon, anesthesiologist, and anyone else who might need your medical information.

It's all part of an organized effort at modernizing the $1.9 trillion U.S. health care system, which to this point has largely run on paper. In fact, President Bush set 2014 as the target for all Americans to have electronic records. But while recording and exchanging patient information electronically saves providers time and money, it also makes it easier for criminals to gain access to private medical files.

What's it costing our system?

Approximately 3% (or $60 billion) of all U.S. health care costs result from fraud, 1% (or $600 million) of which results directly from medical identity theft.

The more people who have access to your files, the greater your risk of fraud or misuse.

In addition to medical professionals, insurance companies, marketers, or anyone else with an interest in your medical history can get some—if not all—of the information in your files. The payment trails from hospitals and pharmacies through to insurance companies and employers create many opportunities for wrongdoers to get their hands on your sensitive data.

Someone who reads through your files can learn quite a bit about you; not only your name, birthday, and address, but your lifestyle, health concerns, and even your family's medical history. The files may represent years' worth of information gathered from doctors, nurses, dentists, psychologists, and more. They'll show whether you smoke, have kids, have ever had surgery, or whether your family has a history of cancer. Readers will also

USA TODAY Snapshots®

Electronic health records face security questions

The U.S. government wants electronic health records available to most U.S. citizens on a voluntary basis by 2014. What is the top challenge to meeting this goal?

Overcoming privacy and/or security issues **44%**
Complexity and cooperation within the health industry **24%**
The cost to taxpayers **15%**
Lack of national focus due to changing politics **14%**
Don't know **3%**

Source: Healthcare Consumer survey of 1,095 adults 18 and older conducted by Health Industry Insights, IDC. Margin of error ±3 percentage points.

By Jae Yang and Bob Laird, USA TODAY 2006

see the results of any blood tests or laboratory tests you've had, as well as what medications you take. If you've ever applied for disability or life insurance, this may also be in your files.

When Hospital Workers Are the Problem

Doctors' offices, clinics, and hospitals are a fruitful hunting ground for identity thieves, who are using increasingly sophisticated methods to steal patient information, lawyers and privacy experts say.

Recent disclosures that hospital workers snooped into the medical files of Maria Shriver, Britney Spears, and George Clooney highlight the vulnerability of patients to the merely curious and the criminal.

Legal experts say lawbreakers use medical information to get credit card numbers, drain bank accounts, or falsely bill Medicare and other insurers.

Marc Rotenberg, executive director of the Electronic Privacy Information Center, says attention on identity theft has focused on how easily criminals can get financial records. "Now we're moving into an era where many of those same problems occur with medical records," he says.

Hospitals and other medical settings often encrypt data and take other steps to protect privacy, but "people are acting with increasing sophistication to steal information," says Stuart Gerson, a Washington, DC-based attorney who represents health care firms.

Pam Dixon, executive director of the World Privacy Forum, an advocacy group, says, "If you steal someone's medical identity, then multiply that by 100 or 1,000" other thefts "and do fake billings, you can make hundreds of thousands, if not millions, of dollars."

In Florida, a front-desk coordinator at the Cleveland Clinic was convicted of identity theft, computer fraud, and other charges after downloading patient information and selling it to a cousin, who submitted more than $2.5 million in phony bills to Medicare.

When Hospital Workers Are the Problem, cont'd

A former New York-Presbyterian Hospital employee was arrested for participating in an identity theft scheme in which he allegedly accessed nearly 50,000 patient records over two years.

False information from fake billings can end up in patients' medical files—and creditors might seek payment from the patients. Until the creditors call, patients might not know their medical information has been accessed.

In a recent survey of 263 health care providers, 13% said their facility had experienced a data breach. Of those, 56% said they notified the patients involved, according to the survey by HIMSS Analytics, a nonprofit data analysis firm, and Kroll Fraud Solutions, which offers security-related services.

 "Identity thieves prey on patients' medical records," by Julie Appleby, May 7, 2008.

What protections federal law (HIPAA) offers

The Health and Insurance Portability and Accountability Act of 1996 (HIPAA) was passed to protect the privacy of health records and prevent identity theft. The goal of HIPAA is to give individuals the right to decide who can and cannot access your medical records (including medical data, suggested treatment plans, medical billing information, and sensitive data collected and stored by your insurance companies). If you've been to a doctor in the last few years, you're probably somewhat familiar with HIPAA, having had to fill out a form saying who can see your records or receive phone messages about your care. Let's look at how well the law lives up to its goals.

All health care providers, including doctors and insurers, must follow HIPAA regulations and policies, which include the following:

- you have the right to receive a copy of your medical files

- you have the right to correct any errors on your files
- health care providers cannot release your health records (for marketing purposes or otherwise) without your consent, and
- health care providers must clearly inform you of how they're sharing and using your personal health information.

One large loophole is mostly used by marketers. Your health care providers are allowed to send you, without your consent, information on managing existing conditions (such as tips for maintaining normal blood pressure), or information on new health care developments, and announcements of new services at a medical facility. These open many doors of opportunities for marketers to target audiences based on their medical records.

Another problem is that some medical information is not covered by HIPAA, including information found in your financial records, school records, and employment files. Any health information that finds its way into these files is largely unprotected.

USA TODAY Snapshots®

Overseeing health records

A transition to electronic medical records is one of the top concerns in the health care industry in the next 12 months. Should electronic medical records be run by the government?

Yes **13%** — No **87%**

Source: Picis survey of 300 physicians, nurses and hospital administrators

By Jae Yang and Julie Snider, USA TODAY 2008

Once your medical information is in the hands of retail companies, schools, and other, nonhealthcare companies, it's no longer protected by HIPAA. The more databases you're in, the more likely it is that your information will be sold, traded, and possibly even stolen.

Adding fuel to this fire is the fact that no law today gives victims of medical identity theft the right to put a fraud alert on their health care files to prevent the crime from happening again. While victims of financial identity theft can put a security freeze on their credit reports, victims of medical identity theft face the daunting task of finding, analyzing, and correcting all their health records. And then they must carefully monitor their files, rather than simply freezing them. This process can go on for years, especially if a thief continues to misuse a victim's information.

A Three-Year Nightmare

When Valley Medical Center sent 29-year-old Jessica an emergency room bill for $23,000, she knew something was wrong. She'd never even heard of Valley Medical Center, and the last time she'd been in an emergency room was when she was a teenager.

Jessica called the hospital and told them that there must be a mistake. However, they confirmed that someone had checked in using her name, date of birth, and Social Security number. They demanded that she pay her bill or be sent to a collection agency. She was devastated. She'd spent years building up her good credit, and planned to buy a house in the next year.

Fortunately, the police were able to find the perpetrator. An undocumented immigrant had purchased Jessica's identity a year before and used it to get a job at a nearby restaurant. When the immigrant got into a car accident, she gave the hospital Jessica's information to get medical help.

Still, Jessica spent many hours convincing the hospital that the bill was not hers, and getting the imposter's medical information removed from her files. Start to finish, it took three years to resolve her ordeal.

Who really needs access to your medical data

In most cases, you have control over who can and cannot see your medical records. However, if you want to obtain health care, qualify for insurance, or be hired for a certain job, you may have no choice but to release this information to the following groups:

- **Insurance companies,** which will normally evaluate your health records before issuing a new policy or making a payment under an existing policy. Insurance companies are legally considered financial institutions, meaning that they must tell you how they obtain and use your customer information. You may be able to opt out of sharing some information with other companies. Contact the National Association of Insurance Commissioners (www.naic.org) for more information on your rights (laws vary by state).

- **Government agencies,** which require your medical records in order to investigate claims made through Medicare, state agencies like MediCal (in California), disability services, and other government agencies.

- **Employers,** which may ask employees to disclose their medical records—often through an employment background check.

- **Direct marketers,** which may obtain your medical information if you participate in informal health screenings. For example, many companies offer free or low-cost cholesterol, blood pressure, weight, and fitness tests at your local mall, community center, or even your workplace. Your results may end up in the databases of companies that sell services and products related to these conditions.

Whether to store your medical files online

You may have seen ads for Internet storage services, encouraging you to store personal health records (PHRs) online. Microsoft and Google are among the companies that give consumers an online portal to manage their digitized information and share it with their health care providers (for free). The idea has many advantages, especially for people who've moved or changed doctors a lot. No longer will you have to remember what drug it was that gave you that bad itch, or when you had your last tetanus vaccination.

But these services come with privacy risks, especially when you consider that technology companies, unlike health care companies, are not subject to HIPAA. (They're exempt because they store data on behalf of consumers, not health care providers.)

However, most of these online health services have stringent user privacy and data security policies and measures, which give you control over access to their information. Google and Microsoft have both promised consumers control of their medical information. Nevertheless, without legislative protection, only you can decide whether you trust these companies and others like them to access your entire medical history. And despite their best efforts, there's always the risk of security or data breaches.

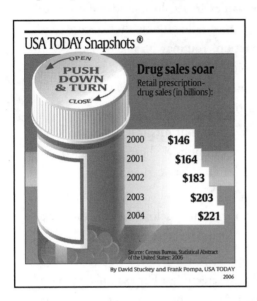

USA TODAY Snapshots®

Drug sales soar
Retail prescription-drug sales (in billions):

2000	**$146**
2001	**$164**
2002	**$183**
2003	**$203**
2004	**$221**

Source: Census Bureau, Statistical Abstract of the United States: 2006

By David Stuckey and Frank Pompa, USA TODAY 2006

Carefully read the privacy policies on company websites before signing up, as they're constantly reviewing and readdressing privacy issues. You might decide that the benefits and conveniences offered by digitized records are worth the privacy tradeoffs. Or you might choose to wait until these companies have a longer track record of responsibly storing your valuable files.

Preventing Medical Identity Theft

Unless you want to pay for someone else's appendectomy, here are ways to protect yourself from medical identity theft:

- **Get familiar with your health care providers' privacy and security policies.** Where are your (and your children's) records stored? How is your identity verified when you check in? Some health care providers do little more than observe the basic regulations found in HIPAA. At a bare minimum, make sure your provider requires photo identification, as well as insurance cards, for nonemergency treatment. If you have concerns about your providers' practices, raise these concerns during your visits.

- **Don't waive too much.** When you're asked to sign a waiver for the release of your medical records, limit the amount of information that can be released. Rather than signing a complete waiver, specify your preferences. For example, your waiver may read "I authorize any physician or medical professional to release to insurer any information regarding my medical history or tests." Cross this out and write "I authorize Dr. XTZ to release to XYZ Insurance Company only information regarding my treatment on XYZ date for XYZ condition."

USA TODAY Snapshots®

Price of sickness rising
Average prescription-drug price (in dollars):

$46 $50 $55 $60 $64

2000 2001 2002 2003 2004

Note: Average of brand and generic drugs
Source: Census Bureau, *Statistical Abstract of the United States: 2006*

By David Stuckey and Marcy E. Mullins, USA TODAY
2006

- **Don't reveal too much online.** When visiting health-related websites and participating in online discussion groups, make sure you understand how the information you provide will be used and protected. The downside of providing any identifying information (such as your name, address, and details about your medical history) online is that if this information were somehow accessed, you could become a victim of medical identity theft, or experience job loss or insurance cancellation. Provide only the minimum amount of personal information necessary to register.

- **Don't rush to free health screenings.** Before participating in health screenings offered in shopping malls and other public places, find out what uses will be made of the medical information that's collected. If you're not given the opportunity to say "no" to the sharing of your medical information with others, don't participate.

Spotting and Curing Medical Identity Theft

Many people find out the hard way that someone else has appropriated their medical identity. For example, you could apply for medical benefits but be denied because someone else is already receiving them in your name. Or you could apply for life insurance and be turned down because an imposter was diagnosed with a life-threatening disease while using your information. And let's not forget the financial consequences—medical identity theft victims are often hit with enormous medical bills that don't belong to them.

Here's what to do before matters go this far:

- **Regularly check your medical records for inaccurate information.** Be alert anytime your doctor reads wrong information out of your file, such as "I see you've had a lung removed." Immediately follow up on any unusual information listed. Realize, however, that while your doctor will no doubt want to gather accurate data, medical institutions as a whole have no legal obligation to correct mistakes. If they refuse to make your corrections in their system, you may submit a formal, written disagreement, which must be included in your file.

- **Keep a close eye on your financial statements.** Your bills and statements may contain important signs that your identity has been misused, such as bills for medical services you didn't receive or notices from doctors you haven't visited. Open and carefully review each medical document you receive. If something looks suspicious, call your provider or billing company right away.

- **Once a year, request a listing of all benefits paid in your name by your health insurer.** The process of requesting and obtaining your medical records can be time consuming and expensive, but it can help you identify serious medical identity theft issues. If you see payments you don't recognize, follow up with the insurer or provider.

- **Keep a running list of any medical services you receive.** That will give you an easy reference guide if an issue arises.
- **Keep an eye on your credit report.** The first warning for many victims of medical identity theft is when their report lists a collection notice from a hospital or medical service provider (especially in cases where the thief has used a different address). Investigate any suspicious items.

If you do become a victim of medical identity theft, be prepared: You'll probably have to correct your information more than once, in more places than you'd expect. For example, one victim, whose medical identity was stolen by a woman to cover her childbirth, thought she'd done everything possible to erase the imposter's details from her medical records. But a few years later, she checked into a local hospital and found that the thief's blood type was still listed in her file. ●

Watch Your Family's Back

I f you have children or elderly parents, the fact that they themselves aren't taking out loans or using credit cards might lead you to assume they'll fall under the radar of identity thieves. Unfortunately, the opposite is true.

Kids are now the fastest growing segment of identity theft victims. More than 10,000 children had their identities stolen in 2006 alone, nearly a 60% increase over 2003. And many more cases may remain undiscovered, because until the child turns 18, no one may think to check his or her credit report. In many cases, the thief is a family member or someone close to the family. Other children's identities are stolen by complete strangers.

Elderly adults are also popular targets, because identity thieves know that they don't check their credit reports often and are likely to have savings, investments, and good credit to draw on. People over age 50 now make up approximately 20% of all identity theft victims.

To protect every member of your family, you need to stay a step ahead of today's fast-paced thieves. This chapter will brief you on what you need to know. While we're at it, we'll cover two other close-to-home topics: whether identity theft insurance (part of many homeowners' policies) is worthwhile, and how to make sure a thief doesn't defraud you out of home ownership.

USA TODAY Snapshots®

Parental rules influence kids online

Kids whose parents set rules governing online use are less likely to do the following:

■ With parental rules □ Without parental rules

Surf the Web
63%
87%

Buy something
19%
55%

Download software
19%
52%

Download music without paying a fee
16%
47%

Source: Harris Interactive for Business Software Alliance; March 14-19 online survey of 1,196 youths ages 8 to 18; margin of error: ±2.8 percentage points.

By Cindy Clark and Karl Gelles, USA TODAY
2007

Too Young for a Plummeting Credit Score: Kids and Identity Theft

Like most ten-year-olds, Chloe spends her days playing with friends and doing her homework. She barely knows what a Social Security number is—yet she is a victim of child identity theft. The thief, an employee at her school, sold Chloe's clean identity to an undocumented immigrant and also tried to open a credit card account in her name.

From the day they're born, children's personal information can be exposed to the world through birth announcements, Social Security applications, and medical forms. With no negative credit history and perfect financial records, a child's personal information is a thief's dream. What's more, it will likely be years before the theft is detected, as most children don't request loans or take other actions that would cause someone to run their credit reports. And, incredibly, lenders and credit reporting agencies don't always check applicants' ages, meaning thieves can use children's identities in much the same way they do adults'—to get credit cards and loans, disassociate themselves from criminal charges, gain employment, or sell their clean identities on the black market to undocumented immigrants or criminals.

USA TODAY Snapshots®

Kids and cellphones
What kids ages 6-18 say about their cellphones:

Their schools have rules restricting cellphone use — 75%

They use their phones for text-messaging — 67%

They've used their phones in an emergency — 50%

Source: Weekly Reader Research

By David Stuckey and Sam Ward, USA TODAY
2007

Chloe was lucky: Her parents were alerted to the crime before any long-term damage was done. However, some child victims are not so lucky. One thief used a seven-year-old boy's name, Social Security number, and clean credit history to purchase a $40,000 houseboat. The child didn't find out about the theft until he was 17, when he applied for a job and a student loan, and was turned down for both due to bad credit.

Child identity theft can harm parents, too. Sean, a father in New York City, couldn't claim his son Miles on his tax returns or receive an economic stimulus payment for him because someone had used Miles's Social Security number to file fraudulent tax returns. Miles was also denied state-sponsored child health insurance because of the identity theft. It took Sean 18 months to clear up the mess, costing him about $2,000.

Resolving a situation that started years ago can be especially messy. Take the typical situation in which the thieves create new credit card accounts for child victims. That's different from most cases of adult identity theft, where thieves prey on existing accounts. With no regular monthly statement to clue the victim in, such new account fraud not only takes longer to detect, but also takes more time and expense to correct. By the time anyone finds out about it, the merchants who sold certain goods may be out of business, and the debts may have been turned over to collection agencies.

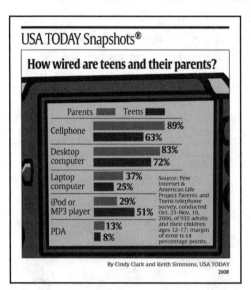

USA TODAY Snapshots®

How wired are teens and their parents?

Parents / Teens

	Parents	Teens
Cellphone	89%	63%
Desktop computer	83%	72%
Laptop computer	37%	25%
iPod or MP3 player	29%	51%
PDA	13%	8%

Source: Pew Internet & American Life Project Parents and Teens telephone survey, conducted Oct. 23-Nov. 19, 2006, of 935 adults and their children ages 12-17; margin of error is ±4 percentage points.

By Cindy Clark and Keith Simmons, USA TODAY 2008

Making Dangerous Connections: Kids and the Internet

The Internet offers many learning and entertainment opportunities for children. And they're certainly taking advantage of it. On any given day, your kids might be found doing their homework on the family computer, texting their friends on their cell phones, or playing online games. Unfortunately, many of the risks faced by children on the Internet are the same as those faced by adults (which we described in Chapter 4). In addition, here are some major threats more unique to kids.

Social networking

Social networking sites have become a popular online hangout for teenagers, and are increasingly embraced by younger children, too. Today, it would be difficult to find an American teen who hasn't heard of MySpace, the majority of whose 100-million-plus accounts were created by users between the ages of 14 and 24.

Kids use MySpace and other social networking sites, such as FaceBook, Friendster, and Hi5, to connect with friends and make new ones. They may tell others what they're feeling that day, or get the scoop on the new kid at school or a secret crush. While most social networking activities are harmless, identity thieves target kids through these sites. They seek out their personal information such as names, birthdays, and where the children go to school.

Most parents are concerned about the online risks faced by their children, especially those related to social networking. And they have good reason to be. One in four kids between the ages of eight and 15 have told surveyors that they allow complete strangers on their social networking friends list, while one in five admitted to meeting up with people they encountered online. A whopping two-thirds of children admitted that they posted information that could help identify them, such as phone numbers and school names.

Such information lets identity thieves create "identity packets," which they then use to conduct pretexting and phishing scams. Personalized scams such as these can be hard even for adults to see through. In fact, the majority of bogus websites used in phishing attacks during the second half of 2007 imitated the log-in pages of two social networking sites.

Online games

Mary knew her 16-year-old son Kevin was a huge fan of online games. He sometimes stayed up until midnight downloading and playing the latest ones with his friends. But she didn't know that some of the games required him to provide personal information to play or to enjoy bonus features.

Mary became suspicious when credit card offers started arriving in the mail under Kevin's name. She started fully investigating when a loan officer called her home to discuss Kevin's application. After a little sleuthing, she discovered that several of the games had required Kevin to fill out applications providing personal details like his full name, birthday, and Social Security number. Eager to play, he'd readily handed over the data, filling out nearly a dozen applications in just a few weeks.

Kevin couldn't remember which sites he'd filled out applications at. Fortunately, he'd been savvy enough to provide a fake birthday and Social

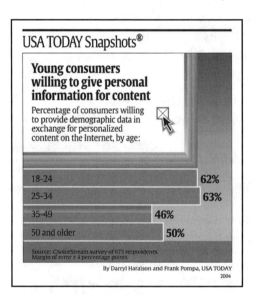

USA TODAY Snapshots®

Young consumers willing to give personal information for content

Percentage of consumers willing to provide demographic data in exchange for personalized content on the Internet, by age:

Age	Percentage
18-24	62%
25-34	63%
35-49	46%
50 and older	50%

Source: ChoiceStream survey of 673 respondents. Margin of error ± 4 percentage points.

By Darryl Haralson and Frank Pompa, USA TODAY 2004

Security number. To be on the safe side, Mary enrolled him in an identity theft protection service, which will alert her if anyone tries to open up a new account in Kevin's name.

Kevin's story highlights the risks faced by children, who may overlook privacy concerns in their quest to enjoy online entertainment. Few kids know enough or take the time to verify a site's legitimacy.

Online gamers are also at risk if they download infected game files. Malware can be hidden in online games, secretly installing malicious files onto your computer when downloaded. When kids play games with others online, they allow numerous users to connect to their computers. An online fraudster can exploit this opportunity to upload infected files or spyware onto your computer, especially if it's not adequately protected with security software. Once infected, the fraudster could track the online behavior of anyone using that computer.

Online Safety Scoop

Marian Merritt, security firm Symantec's Internet Safety Advocate, gives us the scoop on Internet safety practices for parents and children.

Q: How has the Internet changed in the past ten years, and what new risks do these changes bring to families?

A: In the early days of the Internet's growth, the focus was on corporate communications and more direct contact with customers. Since those early, creaky days, we've seen online shopping explode in popularity, online banking mature to become a very useful service, and content creation tools, such as wikis, blogs, and video uploading, simplify to the point where even elementary-school-aged children can use them.

The challenges arise when parents ignore their children's online lives and profess unfamiliarity with the most popular sites and applications. We parents need to get back in the game! That's why I've developed what I call "The Talk," just five easy, nontechnical questions intended to kickstart a better understanding of your child's Internet lives. ("The Talk" is available at www.symantec.com/norton. Under "Community," click "Family Resources," then "How to start the talk on online safety.")

Q: What should parents do to make sure their children are safe and not giving away too much of their personal information on MySpace and other social networking sites?

A: I love social networking. And I encourage parents to sign up for their own accounts. First, you can find out how to make your account more private by reading the instructions under "privacy" on each site. No site is automatically configured for safety by default—you have to take those steps. And then you can show your child how to do the same. Second, you can "friend" your child. Older teens might balk at the idea, but if you tread carefully and

Online Safety Scoop, cont'd

promise not to friend their friends (that can just be weird) and observe but not monitor what they do, it can actually help you to grow closer to your child.

Q: What do parents need to know to protect their children from phishing scams?

A: Kids are increasingly being targeted with phishing scams. That doesn't make sense until you understand that the modern phisher wants more than online banking info. They want usernames and passwords, and your children might have Itunes accounts, online gaming accounts, and other activities of financial value. We've also seen children have their passwords stolen and their social networking profiles hacked or their gaming accounts transferred. Parents need to teach their children never to reply to messages in their favorite gaming site or from friends asking for account or password information. If your child thinks they might have done so, make sure they know you won't punish them, but act quickly to change the password to protect their account.

How to Defend Your Kids

Early awareness of the risks and alertness to the signs of identity theft is critical to preventing long-term damage to your child's credit and good name. Numerous red flags indicate a potential theft, including receiving preapproved credit offers addressed to your child or calls from a collection agency in which the caller asks for your child by name. Other warning signs include notices addressed to your child from the IRS, law enforcement agencies, a department of motor vehicles, or public utility companies.

Here are some ways to limit the opportunities a thief has to steal your child's identity, whether in the online realm or the real world:

- **Avoid giving out your child's Social Security number unless necessary.** Make sure that medical facilities take proper precautions with your child's information, and complain if your child's school uses Social Security numbers to identify students.

- **Shred all papers that contain your child's personal information before throwing them out.** You hopefully do the same for your own papers, so why not do it for your kids?

- **Monitor incoming mail in your child's name.** Credit card offers or even debt collection notices may not be random consumer mailings—they may indicate that someone has been taking out credit in your child's name. If you see anything unusual, contact the sender to find out where they got your child's information.

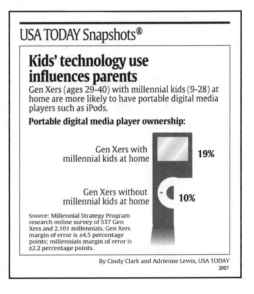

USA TODAY Snapshots®

Kids' technology use influences parents

Gen Xers (ages 29-40) with millennial kids (9-28) at home are more likely to have portable digital media players such as iPods.

Portable digital media player ownership:

Gen Xers with millennial kids at home — 19%

Gen Xers without millennial kids at home — 10%

Source: Millennial Strategy Program research online survey of 537 Gen Xers and 2,101 millennials. Gen Xers margin of error is ±4.5 percentage points; millennials margin of error is ±2.2 percentage points.

By Cindy Clark and Adrienne Lewis, USA TODAY 2007

- **Don't carry your child's Social Security card in your wallet.** If you need to carry a health insurance card with you, and it shows your SSN, carry a photocopied version with the number cut out.

- **Teach your children not to give out personal information without your permission.** As young as is possible, help them understand that the spirit of sharing does not include telling strangers their full name, phone number, or Social Security number.

- **Try requesting your child's credit report.** Hopefully, you'll be told that no such report exists yet, since your child has never applied for credit. But if you get a report, take that as a sign that someone has tried to apply for credit using your child's Social Security number, and follow up accordingly.

- **If your child has a credit report, request a Minor Alert.** A minor alert works like a credit freeze, stopping any third party from getting access to your child's credit report. And it's free upon the request of an adult parent or legal guardian.

- **Talk to your kids about safe computing.** Teach them that some online activities can put them at risk, including clicking on pop-ups, downloading free games, or posting personal information.

- **Set your children's social networking accounts to "Private."** This will ensure that only the people approved as friends will be able to see their profiles. For most sites, you must be logged in to access the "Account" settings, which includes an area for "Privacy." You'll see language like "Who can view my full profile." This is where you can select "Only my friends," or make similar choices.

- **Teach children to be extremely cautious when publishing information about themselves online.** This is especially important if you've allowed them to make their social networking profiles available for anyone to see. For example, personal information like birthdays, full names, phone numbers, and addresses should never be posted on the Internet.

- **Read and follow the safety tips provided by MySpace, Facebook, and other social networking sites.** Each site has its own privacy practices and policies. If your children are heavy users of such sites, you can benefit from knowing how the sites work and discussing the details with your children.

- **Teach your kids to play games only from trusted sources.** Downloading may be tempting, but free software can come with malware.

- **Decide how much you should monitor your children's online behavior.** Various tools are available that let you track your kids' activity online, as discussed in "Finding the Line Between Protection and Obsession," below. Make this a family discussion and decide on the next steps together.

- **Keep the family computer in a public area in the house.** That puts you just a few steps away from potentially seeing what sites kids are visiting. If they're allowed to have computers in their bedrooms, they're more likely to visit risky websites.

- **Encourage your kids to use search engines designed for kids.** Yahooligans (www.yahooligans.com) and Ask for Kids (www.askkids.com) screen out unsavory websites, including those that contain inappropriate language or images.

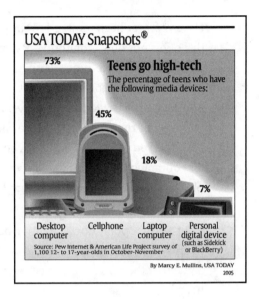

USA TODAY Snapshots®

Teens go high-tech
The percentage of teens who have the following media devices:

73% — Desktop computer
45% — Cellphone
18% — Laptop computer
7% — Personal digital device (such as Sidekick or BlackBerry)

Source: Pew Internet & American Life Project survey of 1,100 12- to 17-year-olds in October-November

By Marcy E. Mullins, USA TODAY
2005

RESOURCE
Guide your kids to more appropriate online experiences.
There are tons of safe, fun, and educational websites for kids today, such as those listed at:

- www.ala.org/greatsites: The American Library Association (ALA) provides a searchable list of safe websites for children of all ages.

- www.kidsites.com: A directory of the best safe websites for kids, teachers, and families.

- www.safesurf.com: Lists search engines and websites that are committed to keeping children safe online.

Finding the Line Between Protection and Obsession

Have you ever been tempted to spy on your kids? Today's technology offers not only monitoring or filtering programs to keep kids away from unwholesome websites, but "snoopware" programs that can give you full reports on everything your kids see or do online. You'd have the power to spy on everything from your children's IM messages to their surfing habits to what they posted on MySpace that day. You could also install spy software that copies all ingoing and outgoing emails and then forwards them to you. You can even plug in a keystroke logger and record every word and character your children type.

But at what point does parenting become stalking? This is tough to answer, as the Internet is a known danger zone. Some parents argue that they wouldn't leave their kids alone in a dangerous neighborhood, so why should the Internet be any different? Seventy-two percent of all parents say they monitor their kids' online behavior. Others say that parents should educate their kids about online risks and arm them with the knowledge and tools to make good decisions, and then give them some privacy.

If you're inclined toward monitoring, we advise including your kids in the decision-making process. Let them know that you're concerned about their safety, and that they can come to you with questions or concerns.

Then choose tools that fit your family's needs and values. For example, if you suspect that your child is engaging in unsafe activities, you can find tools that monitor your child's online activities, block your child's personal information from being emailed or posted online, or filter inappropriate websites, words, and images.

Using spy software programs to track every single thing your kids do online may not be the best solution. Nevertheless, if your child has a history of making bad choices online, then spy software can help you gain more insight into his or her activities and habits.

College Bound: A Time for Added Caution

As your kids transition to adulthood, the college environment exposes them to new identity theft risks. Part of the problem is that college campuses provide students with many opportunities to sign up for credit cards, promotional offers, and services, all of which require personal information, including names, birth dates, and Social Security numbers. And your child is newly busy with a frenzy of online activities, living in an environment where personal information is flowing freely. He or she may also move from one address to another regularly, and not always keep track of the old mail.

> **The real college experience:**
>
> *Nearly half of college students say they receive credit card applications on a daily or weekly basis; and almost 30% of them throw these applications away without destroying them. Another 30% say they rarely, if ever, reconcile their credit card and checking account balances.*
>
> **Source:** Survey by Impulse Research, for Chubb Group Insurance Companies.

Here are some tips to use—or pass on to your child—as you help pack:

- **Set up a credit card account before the child leaves for college.** Or simply add the child to your own card, so that you can keep tabs on expenses and irregularities. That will reduce the temptation for your child to sign up at one of the credit card company displays on campus, which can expose personal information to a large mass of people.

- **Encourage your child to continue using your address as a permanent address whenever possible.** That reduces the chance of mail with personal information, or unsolicited, preapproved credit card offers going to an out-of-date address. Of course, you'll need to follow through by quickly forwarding any important or interesting mail to your child.

- **Find a safe place for personal information in the dorm room.** If lots of roommates and people are passing in and out, this might require buying a locking file cabinet or, if there's no room, hiding files somewhere clever—the bottom of a laundry bag?

- **Don't leave personal papers stuffed in a backpack.** Backpacks are popular targets for thieves, who know that even if they don't find cash inside, they may find a credit card statement or Social Security number. Some colleges use the SSN as student ID numbers, in which case a student card is all the thief needs.

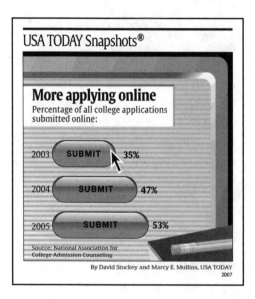

USA TODAY Snapshots®

More applying online
Percentage of all college applications submitted online:

2003 SUBMIT 35%

2004 SUBMIT 47%

2005 SUBMIT 53%

Source: National Association for College Admission Counseling

By David Stuckey and Marcy E. Mullins, USA TODAY 2007

- **Secure the laptop. Colleges are prime hunting grounds for scammers, as many students today use laptops.** Buying a security cable will prevent the laptop from being removed from whatever object it's tied to. In addition, make sure the information inside the laptop is password-protected.

- **Ask your child to at least glance at bank or credit card statements.** If balancing every checking account statement is too much to ask, suggest that your child remember to open bank statements up when they arrive and look for charges—however small—that shouldn't be there. And, of course, your child should learn to open and pay credit card bills as early as possible, to avoid a damaged credit rating even without the help of identity thieves.

- **Remind your child to call home the minute a problem turns up.** That will be your cue to help implement the suggestions in this book.

Even with all these preventive efforts, you probably can't expect your child to never make mistakes. And don't worry, one indiscretion doesn't always lead to identity theft. But it's especially important that you check your college student's credit reports—perhaps every time he or she comes home on a break—following the instructions in Chapter 2.

RESOURCE

Need help with teaching your kids to be financially responsible? You'll find lots of advice—on everything from their first allowance to cutting the cord after they've graduated from college—in *The Busy Family's Guide to Money*, by USA TODAY money experts Sandra Block, Kathy Chu, and John Waggoner (Nolo).

Venerable Yet Vulnerable: Seniors and Identity Theft

Marcia, a disabled senior, first learned that someone had stolen her identity when her credit card company called to tell her that someone had tried to cash a $600 check in her name at a local store. Fortunately, the check was denied because it exceeded the company's $500 limit. And the credit card company cancelled the account after speaking with Marcia.

But Marcia's nightmare wasn't over. The perpetrator turned out to be her live-in employee Elaine, who had unrestricted access to her documents and mail.

Overwhelmed by the betrayal, Marcia couldn't bring herself to confront Elaine, much less fire her or call the police. So Elaine stayed, until Marcia's daughter and son-and-law flew to Los Angeles and fired her. Elaine neither admitted guilt nor claimed innocence, but spent that afternoon removing her belongings from the house. Among these were stacks of unpaid bills, pawn tickets, and frequent-visitor photo-ID cards from local casinos: all clues to financial troubles and an expensive gambling habit. When Elaine lamented that she had nowhere to store her things, Marcia's son-in-law gave her a list of three nearby storage-rental companies. She thanked him, then drove off.

Marcia's daughter also called the police, and hired a new helper. Weeks later, the credit card company called Marcia again to say that over $5,000 in charges had been made in the past month on a new card taken out on her account, in her name. Forging Marcia's signature, someone had used this card at a hair salon, a car-repair company, a local casino—and one of the three storage-rental places on the list that Marcia's son-in-law had given Elaine. The credit card company chose not to prosecute.

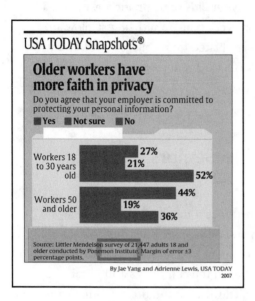

USA TODAY Snapshots®

Older workers have more faith in privacy

Do you agree that your employer is committed to protecting your personal information?

■ Yes ■ Not sure ■ No

Workers 18 to 30 years old
27%
21%
52%

Workers 50 and older
44%
19%
36%

Source: Littler Mendelson survey of 21,447 adults 18 and older conducted by Ponemon Institute. Margin of error ±3 percentage points.

By Jae Yang and Adrienne Lewis, USA TODAY 2007

The police investigation stalled, even after deputies learned of the new charges and even after Marcia had identified Elaine in a photo lineup. With every passing week, the fraud wounded Marcia deeper as she stayed up nights peering out her windows, fearing visits by an armed and furious Elaine. Ultimately, Marcia blamed herself for the fraud, telling people, "This kind of thing only happens to stupid feeble losers."

Investigations on Marcia's case are still pending, and the intervening months have brought more revelations of misbehavior. Friends of Marcia's worry that the psychological and emotional damage might never heal.

Why swindlers love seniors

Cases like Marcia's are increasingly common for elderly men and women. In some cases, the targeting is completely random. However, increasingly savvy criminals have good reason to search out older consumers. Households run by someone 50 years of age or older control more than 75% of the nation's privately held wealth, amounting to about $16 trillion dollars. And as USA TODAY's Sandra Block explains, some seniors can be conned because "They're wary of the stock market and tired of earning less than 3% on a certificate of deposit. Even better, they're often too polite to hang up on a smooth-talking solicitor."

In addition to healthy bank accounts, older consumers have well-established credit, making it easier for thieves to get loan approval in their names. Seniors also have a tendency to carry Medicare cards, many of which still list a Social Security number.

Nursing-home danger zones

Senior citizens in assisted living centers or nursing homes are increasingly targeted by unscrupulous identity thieves—relatives and caregivers among them. Dependence upon caregivers makes the seniors particularly vulnerable to financial fraud, especially when these caregivers have access to their personal and financial records. Examples of crimes targeting nursing home residents include:

- A group of 17 scammers, including nursing home assistants and tax preparers, who teamed up in 2007 to steal the identities of hundreds of nursing-home residents in Kansas City and beyond, using their names to request more than $13.1 million in fraudulent tax refunds.

- In 2007, a woman pre-tending to be a trusted company representative called seniors in several nursing homes and retirement communities and talked them into revealing their personal information. She used this data to open credit card accounts, make purchases, and get cash advances.

USA TODAY Snapshots®

America's oldest age group

Estimated population of Americans 85 and older:

Men — 1.5 million

Women — 3.4 million

Source: Census Bureau   By David Stuckey and Karl Gelles, USA TODAY 2006

- In 2007, a home health aide working at an assisted living facility stole the identity of an 89-year-old resident and used it to run up over $4,000 in fraudulent credit card charges.

How to Protect Your Elderly Family Members

By taking a few simple precautions, you and your senior family members or friends can avoid becoming victims of fraud:

- **Guard the Medicare or insurance number.** Advise your elderly friends or relatives to give these numbers only to people or places that provide them with certified medical services.

- **Leave Medicare cards at home.** If seniors need to carry their Medicare number, make a photocopy of it first, with the last four digits of the Social Security number removed.

- **Watch out for phone and email solicitations.** Advise seniors to never give out personally identifying information (such as Social Security numbers and bank account numbers) via telephone or email. Explain that caller ID can be spoofed by smart identity thieves—so even if the display says "Bank of America," that doesn't mean it's really your bank calling.

- **Don't leave clues in the trash.** Make sure your senior family member has a shredder, and knows how to use it to shred any personal mail and receipts.

- **Beware of medical identity theft.** Check medical files regularly to make sure they're accurate, and keep a close eye on the insurance statements. Read Chapter 8 for more details on how to prevent medical identity theft.

- **Request credit reports.** Check seniors' credit reports regularly and follow up on any mistakes or unfamiliar items (Chapter 2 will guide you through this process). If you're doing this on an elderly relative's behalf, that person will need to provide a Social Security number and answer some questions to confirm his or her identity in order for you to pull the report.

- **Ask about care-center procedures.** If the senior lives in a nursing home or assisted living center, ask the provider to describe the precautions taken to protect residents' private information (including Social Security numbers) and ensure that only the people who truly need this information can access it.

- **Take extra steps as elderly relatives become less able to act for themselves.** You, or whoever is serving as financial power of attorney, will need to carefully monitor their mail, especially bank and charge card account statements, to ensure that no unexpected bills or charges appear. (For more on powers of attorney, see the free articles in the Nolopedia at www.nolo.com, and see *The Busy Family's Guide to Estate Planning: 10 Steps to Peace of Mind*, by Liza Weiman Hanks (Nolo).)

- **Regularly ask your elderly relative whether he or she has responded to any contacts about lotteries, sweepstakes, or other special offers via email, phone, or snail mail.** Try to verify the offeror's legitimacy with the Better Business Bureau (BBB), and undo any damage.

- **Screen caregivers.** If you hire any nurse aides or other caretakers to care for your elderly relative, make sure they've passed a thorough criminal records and background-screening process. Most reputable home care agencies thoroughly screen, train, and supervise their employees. If you're hiring an individual caregiver or private nurse, you can order a criminal background check through a company like LexisNexis or Intelius. It's also a good idea to request (and call) three professional and three personal references.

Whether to Buy Identity Theft Insurance

Cleaning up the mess if anyone in your family is victimized can be time-consuming and expensive. To help minimize this type of damage, many companies offer identity theft insurance, which generally costs between $25 and $50 per year per person. But is it worth the money?

It's important to understand that identity theft insurance cannot protect you from becoming a victim of identity theft—no one can guarantee this. What's more, most policies don't cover direct monetary losses, such as money stolen from your bank account, or debt incurred on your credit card. What this insurance does is to reimburse you for costs related to repairing the damage, such as the costs of making phone calls and photocopies, mailing documents, taking unpaid time off work, and paying notary and attorney fees.

Identity theft insurance can be purchased as a stand-alone policy or in one of the following ways:

- **With your homeowners' insurance policy.** Some homeowners' policies include identity theft coverage to customers at no extra cost. Others allow you to purchase it as an optional extra.

- **Through your credit card company.** Many credit card companies offer identity theft insurance or protection as an optional service to members.

Many consumer advocates argue that identity theft insurance isn't worth the money. For example, *Consumer Reports* included identity theft coverage on its list of "10 insurances policies you don't need." However, others say that, for a small premium, insurance gives consumers some peace of mind.

If you decide that identity theft insurance is right for your family, check with your homeowners' insurance provider and credit card companies first to see whether they offer it free or as inexpensive add-on. If you decide to purchase an insurance policy, shop around and ask five important questions:

- **What are the policy's limits?** Maximum payouts typically range from $10,000 to $25,000.

- **Is there a deductible?** Some policies require that you pay $100 to $500 out of pocket before your coverage kicks in.

- **What does it cover?** Attorney fees and lost wages will likely be your biggest expenses, so choose a policy that includes these.

- **Who is protected?** Just you, or your entire family?

- **When does coverage start?** If you discover your identity has been stolen after buying the insurance, but the actual crime occurred before the purchase, are you still covered?

Guarding Ownership of Your Home

As if stealing money using your credit and bank accounts weren't enough, some identity thieves are now targeting your family's home. The Federal Trade Commission (FTC) has received thousands of real-estate-related identity theft complaints over the past few years. And while still relatively rare, the problem is growing, especially in high-risk states like Arizona and California.

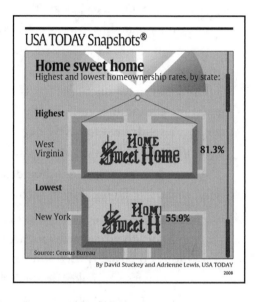

USA TODAY Snapshots®

Home sweet home
Highest and lowest homeownership rates, by state:

Highest

West Virginia — 81.3%

Lowest

New York — 55.9%

Source: Census Bureau

By David Stuckey and Adrienne Lewis, USA TODAY
2008

What exactly are the thieves up to? Some steal a person's identity to take out loans or rent properties (so at least it's not your home and hearth they're laying claim to). Others, however, actually steal homeowners' properties right out from under them, by gathering enough personal information to create fake identity documents, then forging their signatures on title deeds and financial documents.

For example, the thief might prepare a quitclaim deed in your name, transferring the property to the thief. (A quitclaim deed is used by one person to disclaim any interest in an asset and transfer the ownership to another person.) This deed has to be signed in front of a notary public, but that's where the fake IDs come in (or some thieves work with crooked notaries). The thief then typically resells the property to an unwitting buyer, and disappears with the money.

Homeowners might find out about such frauds only when they try to refinance, take out a home equity loan, or face an eviction notice or an eager real estate agent. One homeowner, for example, had to convince a real estate agent that he was not, as the identity thief claimed, merely squatting in the thief's house. Others have come home from vacation to find someone else living in their house.

Home equity loans are another hot target for identity thieves. Unlike mortgage loans, the documentation required for a home equity loan is a piece of cake. Many loan applications are processed remotely, and identification is rarely required. By combining stolen financial information with forged or stolen documents, identity thieves have convinced lenders that they are the actual homeowner, and taken out a home equity loan—backed by the victim's home.

If you fall victim to such fraud, the burden of proof will be on you to prove ownership of your home. Proving that someone stole your information to conduct false transactions can be extremely costly and time-consuming, and you may not get much help from the authorities—this is a relatively new crime problem, and in most areas, resources haven't been devoted to it.

Awareness is currently your best defense. Here are a few tips to reduce your chances of falling prey to such a scheme:

- **Look twice at any unfamiliar loan correspondence.** If you receive bills or other financial statements from a mortgage company you don't do business with—in your name or someone else's—don't assume it's a mistake. Read the documents carefully and contact the mortgage company for details.

- **Don't part with sensitive information.** If you receive mail, email, or phone calls from lenders or other companies saying they need your personal information in order to help or serve you, just say no. Many scammers promise special "offers" to help you with your mortgage, or pose as legitimate organizations to con you into handing over your financial details. If an offer sounds tempting, do your homework first. Verify the legitimacy of the company with the Better Business Bureau, and read the fine print before you sign anything.

- **Once a year, check with your local recorder of deeds.** Back when you bought the house, the deed naming you as owner was filed here. It also describes how much you bought it for, and lists any mortgages on the property. Make sure that the information in your file is correct. If someone has taken out a fraudulent loan or mortgage on your home, you'll likely find it here. ●

Have a Safe Trip

A re you getting ready to enjoy some well-deserved vacation time? Or gearing up for an important business trip? If so, you're probably focused on your trip, and trying to forget the cares and stresses of normal life. But when you're away from home, especially overseas, your vulnerability to someone stealing your identity may increase.

So how can you enjoy your vacation or business travels while protecting yourself against identity theft? Here, we'll discuss some things you can do before, during, and after your trip.

> **TIP**
> **Read up on local tourist scams.** Many travel books and websites alert tourists to the most common scams in various destinations. They'll also tell you what you can do to protect yourself while visiting that particular spot.

Booking Your Trip: Don't Get Caught in a Scam

The Internet is full of great travel advice, discounts, and booking opportunities—and also scams. In 2006, for example, a discount travel site offered college students the opportunity to volunteer in South Africa for just a fraction of the regular trip price. Hundreds of students signed up online and paid their money. They got suspicious when they never received an electronic itinerary, and tried to contact the company. The website had entirely disappeared and the phone was disconnected. While the credit card companies eventually reimbursed the

USA TODAY Snapshots®

Online travel purchases
About 79 million U.S. consumers rely on the Internet for travel planning. Most of them, 65 million, purchased travel products/services online. What they bought:

Airline ticket — 56%
Lodging — 49%
Rental car — 26%
Tickets for cultural event — 21%
Tickets for theme/amusement park — 15%

Note: Multiple responses allowed
Source: Travel Industry Association of America and USDM.net survey of 1,300 respondents. Margin of error ±3 percentage points

By Jae Yang and Suzy Parker, USA TODAY
2006

students, this fraudulent company now has their personal information, increasing their risk of future identity theft.

In another travel-related scam, Heather and Nick posted their vacation home for rent online for $4,000 per month, and got an emailed response from an English couple asking whether their home was available for the month of January. The couple explained that they were in the military and unable to get to a bank, but promised to pay $5,000 if Heather and Nick would accept a cashier's check for $10,000, which they could cash and then send the excess to the agent that would be responsible for their transportation.

USA TODAY Snapshots®

European countries we most want to visit

United Kingdom 56%
Ireland 42%
Germany 41%
France 45%
Italy 59%

Note: Respondents could choose more than one country.
Harris Interactive online survey for SideStep of 3,078 adults (Jan. 17-19). Margin of error ±3.8 percentage points.

By Mary Cadden and Sam Ward, USA TODAY
2006

Does this scam sound familiar? It's a variation of the Nigerian money scam, which you learned about in Chapter 5. Heather and Nick cashed the check, sent $5,000 to the couple, and never heard from them again. Days later, their bank called and informed them that the check had bounced.

In yet another variation, scammers sometimes set up phony airfare websites to attract customers by offering discount airline ticket prices. If you submit your credit card information to one of these sites, it will be captured and used to make purchases in your name. Or the site may tell you that your credit card transaction has been declined, and instruct you to wire funds to pay for the tickets.

If you're considering taking advantage of an online or telephone travel offer, check the travel companies with the Better Business Bureau (BBB) and the company's state attorney general's office before you do business. The best way to avoid scams is to use only known and trusted travel companies.

Travel Fraud Gets Technical

At the American Society of Travel Agents' first travel fraud conference nearly two decades ago, one popular scam promised a $29 airfare to Hawaii. The fine-print catch: a required stay at an overpriced hotel.

Variations of that con game, some pitched via the Web or cell phone text messages instead of by telemarketers, are still tripping up unwitting vacationers, experts said at the agents' 2005 panel in Washington, DC.

But the biggest danger facing would-be travelers is the growing threat of identity theft.

Though reports of travel-related fraud have decreased for the past three years, complaints about electronic heists of credit card numbers and other personal data now make up more than one-third of all those filed to the Federal Trade Commission's consumer protection bureau, the FTC's Eileen Harrington says.

And identity theft, which often is facilitated by downloading spyware through pop-up Internet ads that frequently target vacationers, "threatens to undermine everyone's confidence about electronic commerce," Harrington says.

But while electronic theft through spyware and "phishing" schemes that solicit personal information in official-looking email and websites may be a new menace, vacation-certificate scams are "alive and kicking" despite new laws aimed at curbing telephone solicitation, says Noelle Nachtsheim of the National Fraud Information Center. The group offers consumer advice at www.fraud.org.

"Con artists don't care about the law, and they know a lot of people want to speak to a human being (before buying a vacation)," Nachtsheim says. "By using high-pressure tactics on the phone, they're able to influence people in a way pop-up ads could never do."

 "ID theft hooks up with traditional scams," by Laura Bly, March 31, 2005.

Securing Your Home

Thieves of all kinds—those looking for your identity and those simply after your spare cash—tend to break into houses that look unoccupied. And an overflowing mailbox is a particular temptation, as it might contain credit card offers or bank statements with your personal and financial information. Here's how to make sure the thieves pass you by.

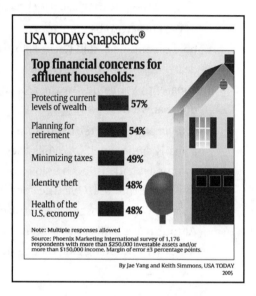

USA TODAY Snapshots®

Top financial concerns for affluent households:

Protecting current levels of wealth	57%
Planning for retirement	54%
Minimizing taxes	49%
Identity theft	48%
Health of the U.S. economy	48%

Note: Multiple responses allowed

Source: Phoenix Marketing International survey of 1,176 respondents with more than $250,000 investable assets and/or more than $150,000 income. Margin of error ±3 percentage points.

By Jae Yang and Keith Simmons, USA TODAY
2005

- **Make it look like you're still at home.** For example, bring trash cans in off the street (or ask the neighbors to do so after a pickup) and leave a light or two on in the house—preferably on a timer.

- **Consider getting a housesitter.** This will certainly make the house look lived in, and mean there's someone there to deal with unexpected events. Of course, you need to find someone you can trust implicitly—otherwise the housesitter could turn out to be an identity thief!

- **Lock away your valuables.** If you have a safe deposit box, transfer your most precious items and personal documents there. If not, find a hiding place within your house. A locked drawer or safe deposit box is best, but you can improvise, perhaps using your basement or attic. (Just don't forget where you put things.)

- **On your way out the door, lock all entry points.** That includes all windows and doors. Even before that, fix any latches that don't work, and trim away any tree branches that offer easy access to upstairs windows.

Free Security Check-Up

Kevin and Alison had planned the wedding of their dreams for a year. When the big day was finally over, a relaxing honeymoon was the only thing on their minds. But they forgot one important planning detail—vacation security precautions.

"We knew we'd be gone for two weeks, but forgot to put a postal hold on our mail," said Kevin. "Normally this wouldn't be a big deal—our mailbox is big enough to accommodate the mail—but apparently someone saw the growing stack in our box and figured out that we were away."

Kevin and Alison returned from their Caribbean honeymoon to a nearly empty mailbox. While they were a little surprised, they assumed it had just been a slow couple of weeks. Unfortunately, this wasn't the case. Over the course of a few weeks, an identity thief had stolen most of their mail, opened up a bank account in Alison's name, and cashed several checks in her name (many of which were wedding gifts that came by mail).

- **Make provisions for your newspaper and mail.** You can have the post office hold mail until you're back and ask your newspaper to suspend service. Alternately, ask a trusted friend or neighbor to bring in all your mail daily—but realize that people are busy, and may not get around to this until late in the day, or even until the next day. Call the U.S. Postal Service at 800-275-8777 to request a vacation hold or go to www.usps.com.

- **Ask a friend or neighbor to remove the pizza fliers.** Even if you've stopped service on your mail and newspapers, things will appear in your front porch—and unless someone removes them, they'll create an obvious sign that you're away.

- **Freeze your credit.** A credit freeze blocks access to your credit report and score, preventing identity thieves from opening new accounts in your name. You can undo the freeze when you're back, or simply wait until the next time you need to apply for a loan or credit card. (See Chapter 2 for instructions.)

- **Schedule online payments for bills that will come due while you're gone.** It's fast and easy—simply call your bank to find out how to set up temporary online payments. Avoiding having paper statements sent to you while you're away can dramatically reduce your chances of one of your bills falling into the wrong hands.

Packing Smart

Sometimes the biggest packing decisions have to do with the smallest items—like whether it would be safer to wear your diamond engagement ring on the trip, or leave it at home hidden in the flour jar. Some of your decision making will depend on personal choice and the safety of your destination. But here are some general tips for most everyone:

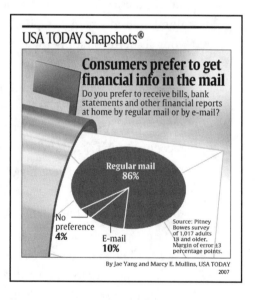

- **Withdraw as much cash as you feel safe carrying.** The safest way to travel is with cash or a combination of cash and traveler's checks. If you don't take enough cash, you may find yourself dependent on an ATM machine that seems shady—and probably is. The more machines have your information stored in them, the greater your risk of identity theft.

- **In case your cash isn't enough:** Research the locations of several local bank branches and print out directions from your hotel to each of them. That will help you avoid ATMs that aren't secure (and you can check out ATM fees, while you're at it).

- **Keep your wallet or purse light.** Bring only one credit card for emergency use, hotel incidentals, and car rentals. And leave your checkbook, Social Security card, library card, and other unnecessary items at home, preferably in a safe deposit box or other secure place.

- **Don't pack your valuables or personal documents in luggage you'll check on the plane.** Always carry your credit cards, traveler's checks, cash, and valuables on your person. In fact, carry these with you to the airplane restroom if you can—thefts have happened from carry-on bags.

- **Make two copies of your passport, driver's license, and credit card.** Take one set of copies with you and leave one with a friend or relative who you can call in an emergency. If your wallet is lost or stolen, these will give you a quick and easy reference for account numbers and emergency phone numbers with which to cancel your accounts or apply for a replacement passport.

- **Decide how you'll pack your laptop.** If you bring one on your trip, make sure it's secure. It should be password-protected (in case of theft), and have the latest Internet security software installed (see Chapter 4). Also consider carrying it in a case that thieves won't recognize, such as a duffel bag instead of a traditional laptop bag.

- **Slip an envelope into your luggage.** This will be handy for collecting credit cards and ATM receipts while you're traveling, so you can dispute any inaccurate charges after you're home and get the bill.

- **Create a list of account numbers, credit limits, and customer service phone numbers for your credit cards.** Bring it with you so you'll know who to contact if your wallet or purse is stolen. The best place to store this list is in your locked hotel safe.

Your Vacation—A Holiday for Thieves?

Identity thieves know that travelers tend to let their guard down, which gives them the perfect chance to steal your identity. Sinead, for example, a 22-year-old student, carelessly left her passport and driver's license in a drawer in her Belize hotel room while she went on a day-long hike. When she returned, the lock on her room was broken and her valuables, including her passport and credit cards, were stolen. She later learned that someone tried to take out a car loan in her name.

USA TODAY Snapshots®

Wallet's lost or stolen while traveling — now what?

Get a cash advance on credit cards **30%**
Wire money through a bank from family/friends **22%**
Borrow money from others traveling with you **15%**
Ask family/friends to send money through a money transfer service **14%**

Source: Western Union survey of 1,000 adults 18 and older. Margin of error: ±3 percentage points.

By Jae Yang and Karl Gelles, USA TODAY 2008

"The hotel room had a safe, but it was broken," said Sinead. "I didn't think twice about leaving my stuff behind. My trip quickly went from playing volleyball and relaxing on the beach to desperately trying to get a new passport and get money sent from home. Next time, I'll be sure to demand a room that has a working safe."

Let's take a closer look at some of the risks and scams that travelers face, from physical theft to dubious ATMs and computer hookups.

Old-fashioned pickpockets and other thieves

One of your biggest risks while traveling is having your wallet or purse stolen. Pickpockets thrive in tourist areas, especially crowded bus stops or tourist attractions. Many are skilled enough to snatch your belongings from your front pockets without you noticing. And they look like everybody else. You could be as easily robbed by the sweet elderly man on the Empire State Building elevator as by the homeless man outside the building.

Many pickpockets use diversion techniques, distracting you just long enough to steal your valuables. For example, many pickpockets work in teams—one person draws you into conversation or asks a question ("What time is it?"), while the other steals your purse. Or a pickpocket might pretend to trip and spill something on you, and then offer to help clean up. In the meantime, the thief also steals your wallet.

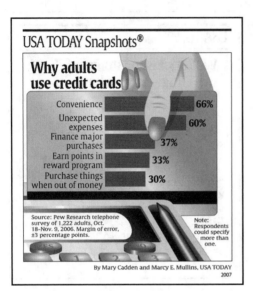

USA TODAY Snapshots®

Why adults use credit cards

Convenience	66%
Unexpected expenses	60%
Finance major purchases	37%
Earn points in reward program	33%
Purchase things when out of money	30%

Source: Pew Research telephone survey of 1,222 adults, Oct. 18–Nov. 9, 2006. Margin of error, ±3 percentage points.

Note: Respondents could specify more than one.

By Mary Cadden and Marcy E. Mullins, USA TODAY
2007

Pickpockets often deliberately bump into their victims, especially in crowded locations where close physical contact doesn't seem odd. In some cases, they carry sweaters or newspapers to hide their hands while they steal your stuff.

Many thieves go beyond your pockets and steal laptop bags, backpacks, and even entire sets of luggage. If you leave your bags unattended—at the airport, bus stop, restaurant, perhaps—your valuables could disappear in just seconds.

Retreating to your lovely hotel can be a relief—except that one of the biggest security problems for travelers is believing that hotels are as safe as their homes. They don't think twice about leaving their laptop or phone in a hotel room, or their bags a few paces behind them in a hotel lobby while checking in. But consider all the people who pass through a hotel, not to mention those who are permitted access to your room when you're not there—hotel managers, housekeepers, bellhops, and more. Any one of these people could steal your belongings and your identity.

Pickpockets May Have Their Eye on You

Beware, all travelers and shoppers. If you're carrying cash or credit cards, roving bands of pickpockets may be casing you now— whether you realize it or not.

"Picking pockets is one of the oldest crimes in the books," says Detective Cedric Mitchell of the Metro Transit Police Department in Washington, DC. "It goes on every day, everywhere."

In recent years, pickpockets and their crews have grown in scope and sophistication, he says. They're no longer clumsy street thugs but slick operators who pride themselves on playing the "game" and "scoring"—stealing a wallet or pocketbook unnoticed, without a gun or knife.

More pickpockets are:

- **Hooking up with crooks who run fast-growing identity theft scams.** Pickpocket gangs will lift credit cards, driver's licenses, and Social Security cards from wallets and purses, then deliver the goods to the identity thieves.

- **Jetting around the country to New York, Chicago, and other big cities they call "hubs," a term swiped from the airline industry.** At the hub cities, they connect with other pickpockets to hang out and trade tips and intelligence on their craft.

- **Following well-heeled crowds to hot vacation spots,** from Florida to Hawaii, or to mega sporting events, such as the Super Bowl, the Olympics, or the World Series.

Usually not violent, pickpockets start as small-time shoplifters or drug users who graduate to working with pickpocket rings around the country, Mitchell says.

The best pickpockets, known as "the cannon" or "the wire," are good enough to go it alone. But most pickpockets work in crews of three or four people.

Pickpockets May Have Their Eye on You, cont'd

Their favorite haunts? Airports, train and subway stations, shopping malls, and other busy gathering spots. They blend in with their surroundings, dressing and acting like others in the environment.

Their favorite victims? Women with loose, dangling purses. Lost out-of-towners or foreigners carrying a lot of cash. Shy, naïve-looking people. Parents distracted by their kids or babies. Well-dressed folks in pricey clothes or jewelry.

Once a target is spotted, the crew tails the victim, then strikes. The first crew member, called "the stall," pretends to drop a coin or a contact lens in front of the victim, who may be riding down an escalator or waiting in a line.

With the victim distracted, a second crew member nabs the wallet or pocketbook. Sometimes, the pickpocket will use a suit bag or briefcase to hide his hand.

Then the pickpocket quietly hands the stolen item to a third gang member, called "the dish," who walks away unnoticed. If the pickpocket is questioned by a suspicious victim or the police, he won't have the goods on him.

All of this happens in an average of four seconds.

 "ID theft hooks up with traditional scams," by Laura Bly, March 31, 2005.

Funny-looking ATMs

You learned about skimmers in Chapter 6—those electronic devices placed over ATM machines to steal your credit card or bank account information. They're not just an American epidemic—they've spread to foreign countries as well. You may already be dealing with a different language and set of customs, so you might not even notice if the ATMs look a little clunky or unusual.

Also, "shoulder surfers"—people who sneak a peek over your shoulder when you enter your PIN—are drawn to high-traffic tourist areas in the hopes that vacationers will be too relaxed to notice their searching eyes. (In some cases, you won't even see their eyes—just the glint of their distant binoculars.) If they get your PIN, they'll try to rob you. If successful, the thief will race to the nearest ATM while you're still looking for the phone numbers with which to cancel your account.

USA TODAY Snapshots®

Where to be Web wary

Places with the most Internet fraud perpetrators, per 100,000 people:

26.5 — Nevada
20 — New York
19.8 — District of Columbia
18.5 — Florida
16.9 — Washington

Source: FBI

By David Stuckey and Alejandro Gonzalez, USA TODAY
2007

Questionable Internet cafés and wireless hotspots

The Internet has become a global lifeline for travelers who want to make sure the housesitter and dog are doing okay, field important questions from the office, or simply access information online.

However, while Internet cafés and wireless hotspots offer many conveniences, many use inadequate security measures, making it easy for thieves to hack your information and steal your passwords. This isn't a problem when you're using the Internet to find the best restaurant or get the phone number of a scuba diving company, but you can compromise your personal data if you use these connections to shop or bank online.

Protecting Yourself While You Travel

When Chris traveled to Costa Rica with two friends after college, she looked forward to a fun and relaxing beach vacation. However, her trip took an unexpected turn when she and one of her friends, Lisa, left their bags with the third friend, Amy, while they used the restroom at a San Jose bus station.

A man sparked a conversation with Amy, and someone else stole Chris's bags while Amy was distracted. "It probably happened in about ten seconds," said Chris. "We came back and our bags were gone."

USA TODAY Snapshots®

Online and outdoors
Percentage of campers who camp with a computer, by age group:

Younger than 35: 20%
35-44: 25%
45-54: 30%
55-64: 40%
65+: 35%

Source: Kampgrounds of America   By David Stuckey and Sam Ward, USA TODAY 2006

The local police weren't helpful, and communication barriers made reporting the crime even more challenging. In addition, the U.S. Embassy was closed when Chris first tried to replace her passport. It took three trips back and forth between San Jose and Manuel Antonio, which are a few hundred miles apart, for Chris to finally get a new passport.

Chris's family back home called her credit card companies to report the crime. It turned out that someone had used her card to run up more than $1,000 in purchases. Fortunately, she wasn't liable for these charges, because of having alerted the credit card company immediately.

"I wouldn't say my trip was ruined, but it turned out to be quite an ordeal," said Chris. "Costa Rica doesn't have Internet cafés left and right, so it wasn't so easy to figure out what to do and where to go for help."

To avoid identity theft while you travel, take these precautionary steps:

- **Use the hotel safe.** Never leave valuables or personal documents like your passport in your hotel room.

- **Use credit cards instead of debit cards.** That protects you from having a thief drain your account, as discussed in Chapter 2.

- **Avoid using checks.** Checking account fraud is one of the most difficult types of identity theft to recover from, and being far from home will only add to your frustration. When traveling, pay for things with cash, traveler's checks, or credit cards.

- **Wear a money pouch close to your body.** Use it to store your money, credit cards, and passport. Keeping these close to your skin (preferably under your clothes), makes it much harder for a thief to steal them. But don't keep all your cash in the pouch—spread it around, with some in your wallet, a little in your suitcase at the hotel, and some in a hiding place of your devising, such as your shoe.

- **Keep an eye on your laptop.** Never let your laptop out of your sight, especially while in an airport, train, or bus station. And don't leave it lying around your hotel room, especially if it has sensitive information on it. Ideally, store it in the hotel safe, instead.

- **Never access personal information, especially bank accounts, from public computers.** Ask your hotel to recommend reputable Internet cafés or Wi-Fi spots before you do any online connecting. And see the suggested protective measures for using public computers in Chapter 4.

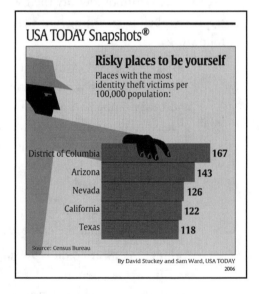

USA TODAY Snapshots®

Risky places to be yourself

Places with the most identity theft victims per 100,000 population:

District of Columbia	167
Arizona	143
Nevada	126
California	122
Texas	118

Source: Census Bureau

By David Stuckey and Sam Ward, USA TODAY 2006

- **Use only ATM machines located inside banks.** While traveling, you'll come across ATM machines in gas stations, conveniences stores, and various other places, but they aren't always safe.

- **Beware of pickpockets.** Keep your radar up for suspicious bumps or efforts to distract you, and keep your hands near your purse or wallet (which is best kept in a front pocket). Keep credit cards and identification is a secure place. If you carry a wallet, avoid keeping any personal information in it.

- **Don't tell the online world you're away.** Many travelers keep family and friends up to date on their adventures by posting to a blog, social network, or photo-sharing service. But look into how private these online communications really are. Don't make it too easy for anyone to figure out that you're not home and target your house for burglary.

- **When using public phones, use a prepaid phone card instead of your credit card.** Shoulder surfers often prey on tourists making credit card calls on public phones.

If You're Victimized on Vacation

By following the steps outlined in this chapter, your vacation should be free of worry, stress, and identity theft. But if bad luck happens and you become the victim of identity theft while traveling, here are your first steps, even before returning home (and see Chapter 11 for additional followup):

- **Cancel your credit cards immediately.** Hopefully, you still have the photocopies of your credit cards with the toll-free phone numbers and card numbers. If not, call whoever you left your copies with, or head to the nearest reputable Internet café or phone booth to get the numbers of your credit card companies. Then call them to report the theft.

- **File a police report immediately, in the area where the theft took place.** Don't wait until you get home, as you may need to show creditors proof that the crime was reported.

- **Contact the three credit reporting agencies—Experian, Equifax, and TransUnion—to place a fraud alert on your credit report.** This ensures that anyone who wants to see your credit report knows your information was stolen and must contact you by phone to authorize any new credit in your name. Don't wait until you get home to do this, as it may be too late.

- **Contact the nearest U.S. embassy or consulate.** The U.S. government says it is "committed to assisting American citizens who become victims of crime while traveling, working, or residing abroad." For locations, see www.usembassy.gov. If your passport was stolen and you're leaving the foreign country soon, inform the embassy of your planned departure date so it can help you obtain a replacement passport quickly. You'll need to provide reasonable proof of your identity, which is where having photocopies of your passport and driver's license comes in handy. If all your personal papers were stolen along with your passport, the embassy may ask to interview witnesses (either people traveling with you or friends and family members at home) to confirm that you are who you say you are.

 TIP

Think you escaped the thieves? Hopefully you're right. Nevertheless, pay special attention to your credit card bills for a few months after you get home, watching for charges that aren't yours. ●

React Quickly If Your Identity Is Stolen

Following the steps in this book will dramatically reduce your chances of becoming an identity theft victim. Still, nothing can guarantee that your information won't fall into the wrong hands. Even if you never divulge your Social Security number to anyone, never click on a suspicious email attachment, and shred everything with your name on it, the matter isn't entirely up to you. Data breaches, new scams, and ever more virulent computer viruses are facts of modern life.

Although becoming a victim of identity theft can be daunting, the good news is that there are many steps you can take to reverse or minimize the damage, as described in this chapter.

Damage Control: Essential First Steps

When you first learn that you're a victim of identity theft, it's natural to wonder how the thief got your information. Was it that time you left your wallet in the restroom at the mall? Did your pizza delivery guy swipe your credit card details? Should you have refused to give your Social Security number at the dentist's office? You may never find out, so let's turn our efforts toward cleaning up the mess, starting with the following steps.

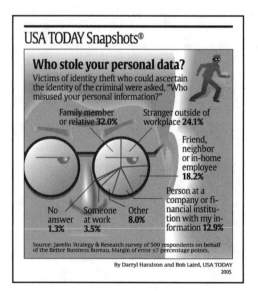

USA TODAY Snapshots®

Who stole your personal data?
Victims of identity theft who could ascertain the identity of the criminal were asked, "Who misused your personal information?"

Family member or relative **32.0%**
Stranger outside of workplace **24.1%**
Friend, neighbor or in-home employee **18.2%**
Person at a company or financial institution with my information **12.9%**
No answer **1.3%**
Someone at work **3.5%**
Other **8.0%**

Source: Javelin Strategy & Research survey of 509 respondents on behalf of the Better Business Bureau. Margin of error ±7 percentage points.

By Darryl Haralson and Bob Laird, USA TODAY 2005

Get organized

Before picking up the phone and scribbling frenzied notes on the back of an envelope, take a few moments to get prepared. And follow the tips below to stay organized as the process continues.

- **Locate your existing files.** You'll need your records from your bank, credit card company, and any other affected account holders. These will help you provide the information you need as you contact people.

- **Set aside a notebook or pad of paper.** You'll use this to keep detailed notes of all conversations, including names, dates, and phone numbers. You'll also want to log the time you spend, for reasons we'll describe below.

- **Start a new file. Label it "Identity Theft [*year*]."** Use it to keep copies of all correspondence and relevant records, such as police reports, fraud forms, fraudulent credit applications, and bills.

- **Keep track of your time and expenses.** If the criminal is ever caught and convicted, the court may (depending on the laws in your state) order what's called "restitution." That means the criminal will, usually as a condition of probation, have to pay you back for your expenses and potentially for your time (particularly if you had to take time off work in order to deal with all this). It's a useful end run around bringing a civil suit against the criminal for the same compensation.

- **Whenever possible, get written proof of your correspondence.** For example, if you send a letter to a credit reporting agency, send it via certified mail.

- **Create a running list of facts about your case.** For example, log the time and place of the theft, list the questions you'd like to ask, and record the answers you receive—including explanations of what you're personally liable for. Don't rely on company representatives to take charge of the process.

- **Follow up in writing with everyone you speak to on the phone.** Your letter should capture what was said during the conversation and what actions were agreed upon. For example, if your credit card representative said he'd start a fraud investigation, state this promise in your letter and request an update on the investigation. Use certified mail so you have proof of the correspondence.

The Long Road Back From Identity Theft

When Jason, a 36-year-old account manager, tried to refinance his home, he was surprised to find out that his credit score was extremely low. A quick review of his credit report revealed that identity thieves had used his name and Social Security number to open up three lines of credit, later written off due to lack of payment. His good credit had been destroyed.

Jason acted quickly, informing police and creditors. Still, clearing his name and credit report turned out to be a long and tedious process.

Jason's story is not unique. And according to a Gartner study, the trend is for identity theft victims to lose more money and get less of it back than ever before. The average loss of funds in a case of identity theft was $3,257 in 2006, up from $1,408 in 2005. In 2005, victims recovered 87% of funds; in 2006, they recovered only 61%.

Nevertheless, the faster you react to an identity theft, the less money and time you'll spend fixing the damage.

Contact credit reporting agencies and request fraud alerts

As soon as you find out you've been victimized, report the crime to Equifax, Experian, or TransUnion, and ask to put a fraud alert on your file. In theory, you need to notify only one CRA to get fraud alerts placed on all three files (they're supposed to notify each other). But just in case, if you don't receive confirmations by mail from all three agencies, contact the remaining two directly.

As discussed in previous chapters, a fraud alert prevents criminals from opening new accounts using your identity. When the thief tries to, for example, take out a loan in your name, the creditor will call you at the number you provided before approving the loan application. While this won't help correct any damage that's already been done, it can drastically reduce a thief's chances of inflicting greater damage. Consider using your cell phone as the fraud-alert contact number, so creditors can reach you more quickly.

You can request a short-term alert, which lasts for 90 days, or an extended alert, which stays on for seven years. You'll need to send proof of identity theft, including an identity theft report, to activate the seven-year report.

Also request that the CRAs add a statement to your credit reports reiterating that potential creditors call you before granting any credit in your name. These statements will remain on your credit reports for seven years.

USA TODAY Snapshots®

Insider attacks increase

Percentage of companies that have had security incidents caused by employees or former employees:

69%

51%

2006

2007

Source:
CIO, CSO and PricewaterhouseCoopers Global State of Information Security 2007 survey of 7,200 CEOs, CFOs, CIOs, vice presidents and information technology professionals. Margin of error ±1 percentage point.

By Jae Yang and Sam Ward, USA TODAY
2008

It's important to understand that these measures will make it more difficult for you to get credit, as well, but this is a good thing. If it's a hassle for you to get a new line of credit on the spot, think of how hard it will be for a thief to do so.

Once you've reported the crime and requested a fraud alert, you'll receive a complimentary copy of your credit report from each of the three CRAs. When they arrive, carefully review them. Go back to Chapter 3 for detailed information on how to thoroughly check your report for errors and red flags. Also double check to see that each credit report includes the fraud alert and your correct telephone number.

Freeze your credit

If your identity has been compromised and you don't want any new credit to be granted in your name, you can ask the CRAs for a credit freeze. This offers more protection than a fraud alert. Once placed, no one can open new lines of credit in your name until you remove the freeze.

You must contact each of the three major CRAs individually with this request. Depending on which state you live in, you may be required to pay fees, although the fees may be waived for victims of identity theft or senior citizens. For more information on how to freeze your credit, read Chapter 2.

Contacting CRAs		
Here's how to reach the fraud departments of the three major credit bureaus.		
Credit Bureau	**Phone Number**	**Website Address**
Equifax	800-525-6285	www.equifax.com
Experian	888-397-3742	www.experian.com
TransUnion	800-680-7289	www.transunion.com

File a complaint with the police

You may hear that filing a police report would be a waste of time, especially if you have no idea how the theft happened or who the thief might be. Indeed, it's unlikely that the identity thief will be caught or even pursued. However, filing a complaint serves another important purpose: It will help you prove your innocence to your creditors and the CRAs.

In a classic insult-to-injury scenario, you may face skepticism when reporting identity theft to the companies who think you owe them money. Lenders will want to see proof that you're an identity theft victim—they've heard similar sounding stories from deadbeats trying to get out of paying their bills. In this situation, a police report can help you prove that your accounts were indeed compromised. To file your report, you can use the Identity Theft Complaint form described in Chapter 3, and available at www.ftc.gov.

Don't get discouraged if the police are less than enthusiastic about catching the criminal. Some police departments dissuade victims from filing police reports. They're busy fighting countless other crimes, and may see your case as one they can't really solve. Be persistent and explain that you need a police report to repair your credit and to stop the theft from doing further harm. Ask for the names and phone numbers of any police investigator working on your case—you may need to give it to creditors and others who require verification.

If your local police department refuses to help you (yes, this sometimes happens), go to another jurisdiction, such as the county or state police. You can also contact your state attorney general's office to find out exactly what you need to do to officially report the crime.

USA TODAY Snapshots®

Remedies for identity theft

How affluent households would counter identity theft

- Fast cancellation of account upon notification: **86%**
- Impose stricter guidelines on opening new account: **79%**
- Help consumers to assess risk level for being victim: **67%**
- Educate consumers on the risks of identity theft: **62%**
- Offer additional ID theft protection for a fee: **20%**

Source: Phoenix Marketing International survey of 1,176 respondents with more than $250,000 investable assets and/or more than $150,000 income. Margin of error ±3 percentage points.

By Jae Yang and Bob Laird, USA TODAY 2005

Once you've filed a police report, be sure to get copies of it—you'll need to send these to creditors. If the police won't provide you with a copy, ask for the report number and a letter stating that the report was filed.

Fill out an ID Theft Affidavit

If an identity thief has opened multiple new accounts using your name, you'll face the task of proving your innocence to several companies, each of which may ask you to fill out lengthy fraud reports. To make things easier, the FTC, along with a group of creditors and consumer advocates, has created the ID Theft Affidavit. Many companies accept this affidavit in place of their individual fraud reporting forms.

The ID Theft Affidavit can help you prove that you're a victim of identity theft. For example, if a thief opened a credit card account in your name but used a different address, it might be difficult to convince the creditor to close the account and remove it from your credit file, as you can't verify the address on file. The affidavit shows the creditor that you are a victim of identity theft and that you are who you say you are.

USA TODAY Snapshots®

To the max

Ten percent of inmates in the Federal Bureau of Prisons' 106 institutions are in high security levels. Percentage of inmates by security level:

Low 40%

Medium 26%

High 10%

Note: Remaining 24% of inmates are in minimum and unclassified levels of security.

Source: Federal Bureau of Prisons By David Stuckey and Bob Laird, USA TODAY 2005

The ID Theft Affidavit is available at www.ftc.gov/idtheft (click "If your information has been stolen and used by an identity thief," and then look under "Close the accounts that you know, or believe, have been tampered with or opened fraudulently").

Before sending the affidavit to a creditor, call first to find out whether the company accepts it. If not, ask what documentation it requires in order to have any fraudulent accounts opened in your name closed and removed from your report.

Contact your "new" creditors

If you discover that new loans, credit cards, bank accounts, or service accounts have been opened in your name, contact the fraud departments of those creditors immediately, by telephone and in writing. They can tell you what forms you need to complete to dispute the fraudulent transactions. Ask whether you can use the ID Theft Affidavit.

Once you've resolved your identity theft dispute with your creditors, request letters from each one, confirming that the fraudulent debts have been discharged. If errors relating to this account reappear on your credit report or if bill collectors contact you about these charges in the future, you'll need all the proof you can muster, to show that this issue was resolved.

New Account Fraud Hits Victims Hardest

Identity theft involving new accounts—whether they're bank, credit card, utility, or car loan accounts—is more expensive and much harder to recover from than identity theft involving existing accounts. The new accounts are opened in your name, but the statements and related correspondence are usually mailed to someone else's address. That lets the thieves run up fraudulent charges for a long time without you finding out about it.

With misuse of existing accounts, an FTC study found that the average loss was less than $500, while new account fraud losses averaged $1,350. In addition, the FTC said that, in cases of new account fraud, victims were more than twice as likely to report having one or more of the following problems:

- harassment by debt collectors
- being unable to get loans
- having their utilities cut off
- being subject to a criminal investigation or civil suit, or being arrested, and
- having difficulties obtaining or accessing bank accounts.

Notify other relevant agencies

Numerous state and federal agencies can help you recover from various types of identity theft. For example, if you suspect that your checks were stolen from your mailbox, notify your local postal inspector. Theft of the mail or using the mail to commit a crime is a felony, and the Postal Service will investigate.

If your passport was stolen, alert your local passport office (administered by the U.S. Department of State, www.state.gov). That warns the agency that the identity thief may apply for a new passport using your identity. You'll need to apply for a new passport.

If your driver's license number has been used to open accounts or validate checks, contact your state's department of motor vehicles. You may need to change your driver's license number and place a fraud alert on your license.

If you're a victim of tax-related identity theft, call the Internal Revenue Service (www.irs.gov) to report the crime.

File a complaint with the Federal Trade Commission (FTC)

Finally, file a complaint with the Federal Trade Commission (FTC), which can be done online at www.ftc.gov/idtheft, or by phone at 877-IDTHEFT. While the FTC doesn't get involved with individual cases, telling it about the crime will help the government compile accurate statistics about trends, and allocate resources for fighting identity theft.

Additional Steps If the Thief Accesses Your Financial Accounts

If you discover that someone has stolen or misused your credit, ATM, or debit card number or PIN, or otherwise found a way to access your brokerage, utility, or other accounts, you'll need to act quickly. Take the following steps:

- **If your card or PIN is stolen, report it to the issuing company immediately.** (Or as soon as you reasonably can, keeping track of the time limits set out in Chapter 3.) Don't delay—call immediately and follow up with a certified letter. Cancel the card and have a new one issued, with a new account number and PIN or password. Follow up with a letter, detailing the date and circumstances of the loss or theft. Send your letter by certified mail, and request a return receipt. It becomes your proof of the date the bank or creditor received the letter. Include copies (NOT originals) of your police report or other documents that support your position. Keep a copy of your letter.

- **If you think someone has stolen your PIN but you still have your card, contact your bank or creditor.** Ask to change your PIN number immediately.

- **Ask to open new accounts with different account numbers.** Guard these with new PINs and passwords.

- **Ask that your old accounts be processed as "account closed at consumer's request."** On your credit report, this shows that the account is not in negative standing.

Additional Steps If You're a Victim of Check Fraud

If your checking account is compromised, it could take days, or even weeks, to get your money back—assuming the bank decides that the fraud is not your fault. Your first step is to carefully read your bank contracts to understand your liability for fraud losses. Pay extra attention to where the bank outlines your responsibilities when managing your checks. For example, most banks require customers to report fraud within a reasonable period of time, typically 60 to 90 days from receiving the bank statement showing the loss. If you fail to do so, you may be stuck with the loss.

The following actions can help limit your loss and clear your good name:

- **Notify your bank of the theft immediately.** Cancel the affected accounts and request new account numbers. Ask the bank to issue you a secret password that is necessary for every transaction. Stop payments on any outstanding checks that you don't recognize.

- **Ask that your old accounts be processed as "account closed at consumer's request."** On your credit report, this shows that the account is not in negative standing.

Report the fraud to the following companies:

- **National Check Fraud Center (www.ckfraud.org),** which provides assistance and support in the areas of check fraud, forgery, counterfeiting, bank fraud, and white collar crimes.

- **TeleCheck (www.telecheck.com),** which will place a fraud alert on your file, alerting banks of the check fraud alert each time they inquire about you. This helps prevents thieves from opening checking accounts in your name.

- **Global Payments Check Services (www.globalpaymentsinc.com),** which will place a fraud alert on your file.

- **Shared Check Authorization Network (800-262-7771),** which will place a fraud alert on your file.

Additional Steps If You're "Wanted" by the Police

Identity thieves aren't exactly law-abiding citizens. Chances are if they've stolen your identity, they may be committing other crimes. And if they're committing these crimes using your identity, you'll find yourself facing a whole other set of problems.

Unfortunately, if someone uses your name to commit a crime, the manner in which you discover it may be shocking and unpleasant. You might first learn of the crime when a potential employer conducts a background check on you. Or you'll find out when pulled over for a traffic violation or other infraction. At that time, the highway patrol officer runs a search of your criminal records files and discovers an outstanding warrant in your name. You may be brought to the police department and booked for whatever crime the police think you committed. If the crime is a felony, the police may even show up at your door.

Clearing your name can be a little tricky. Because no national system exists for removing your name from all criminal justice databases, the process depends on what state and what county you live in. The best place to start is at the police department or court that arrested the identity thief or issued a warrant in your name. Also contact your state attorney general for advice on repairing the damage.

Here are some other guidelines for clearing your criminal record of inaccurate information:

- To confirm your identity, request that the police department take your photograph and fingerprints and make copies of your driver's license, passport, or other photo ID. They can use these to compare against those of the imposter.

- Once you've proven that you're not the criminal they're looking for, make sure the police cancel any warrants.

- If you're actually arrested for a crime you didn't commit, contact a lawyer immediately. Clearing your name of a criminal offense can be much more difficult than straightening out your credit, so you'll need professional help.

USA TODAY Snapshots®

Cybercrime proliferates
How many incidents of cybercrime has your company experienced in the last 12 months?

43% — 1 to 9
8% — 10 to 24
2% — 25 to 49
6% — 50+
22% — None

Source: CSO magazine survey conducted in January of 520 chief security officers and senior security executives. Margin of error ±4 percentage points.

By Darryl Haralson and Alejandro Gonzalez, USA TODAY 2004

- Once you're cleared for the crime for which you are arrested, the police should issue a "clearance letter." Be sure to make copies of this letter and carry one with you, in case you're ever wrongly arrested again.

- Finally, ask the police department to file a record of your innocence with the court where the crime took place. Also ask that the "key name" on the criminal record be changed from your name to the thief's real name, with your name listed only as an alias.

Additional Steps If Your Medical Records Have Been Affected

Most medical identity theft victims find out that they have a problem when they see a summary of benefits from their insurance company or receive a medical bill for services they didn't receive. If this happens to you, immediately contact every health care provider listed on your statements or bills to report errors or signs of fraud.

It's especially important to file a police report. You may need to send copies of this to health care providers, insurance companies, and other organizations to prove that your files have been compromised and need to be corrected immediately.

In many cases, medical offices will simply delete any wrong information from your files when you explain your situation. But this doesn't mean your medical records have been completely fixed. The erroneous information may have been shared with other health care providers, pharmacies, and insurance companies—and, despite the fact that HIPAA requires the record keeper to report the correction to any other organization it shared the original information with, this doesn't always happen. Contact every organization that might have wrong data in its files, and request corrections.

If record keepers are reluctant to remove errors from your records, be persistent. Remind them that the errors may not only harm you, but could make their organizations legally liable for damages. For example, if a doctor's office or insurance company discloses incorrect information about you, you may be able to sue for damages if they failed to comply with HIPAA regulations. If you think your rights have been violated in any way, or if you are dealing with uncooperative record keepers, contact an attorney.

Don't Want the Hassle? Enlisting the Pros

Finding out that you're a victim of identity theft is devastating enough. Realizing how much of your precious time and energy it will take to restore your name and credit may add salt to your wound. You may be spending your nights and weekends writing letters, making calls, deciphering state and national laws, following up with uncooperative agencies and businesses, and more. It can take thousands of dollars and dozens of hours of your time to clear up a fraud and restore your credit.

All of this work to fix a problem that someone else created for you! Yet if you fail to take action, the alternative is grim. You could be turned down for loans, held responsible for paying off accounts you never opened, and even face jail time for crimes committed by someone else in your name.

USA TODAY Snapshots®

More crimes, same money

Although state court prosecutors reported they faced more complex cases and issues in 2005 than in previous years – such as computer crime and identity theft – the budget has barely changed. Median annual budget for state prosecutors' offices (in thousands):

1996	$316
2001	$351
2005	$355

Source: Bureau of Justice Statistics

By David Stuckey and Adrienne Lewis, USA TODAY 2006

Luckily, there are plenty of experts who can help you do the legwork and paperwork required on the path to recovery.

Hire a lawyer

When you're dealing with a complex identity theft case, hiring a lawyer can be invaluable in helping you clear your name. For example, if you're dealing with a criminal or medical identity theft incident, it's extremely important to erase errors from your criminal and medical records. A lawyer can help you navigate the criminal justice system or use medical privacy laws to thoroughly clean up your medical records.

A lawyer can also help you determine whether to take legal action against creditors, credit bureaus, or debt collectors if they're not cooperative in removing fraudulent information from your credit report.

To find a lawyer experienced in such matters, contact the National Association of Consumer Advocates, a nationwide organization of more than 1,000 attorneys who specialize in consumer advocacy and litigation, at 202-452-1989 or www.naca.net.

Identity theft protection and resolution services

Numerous identity theft protection services can help prevent and detect any signs of identity theft. They can dramatically reduce the amount of paperwork and other headaches you have to deal with. Unfortunately, you can't wait until you're a victim to sign up. They won't usually help you clean up messes that started before you became a customer.

But if you want to stop the crime from happening again, identity theft protection companies offer a wide variety of products and services. Look for comprehensive products that offer the broadest range of services. Some will offer services that you can do yourself for free, like placing fraud alerts or getting your credit report. Other services are far more difficult to replicate yourself, like helping restore a lost identity or scanning public records databases and crime reports to find out whether your information is being used suspiciously.

File an insurance claim

If you have identity theft insurance—through your homeowners' policy, credit card company, or as a stand-alone policy—file an identity theft claim immediately. Your policy should tell you what you need to provide, and the insurer may provide a case manager to assist you with contacting authorities, credit bureaus, creditors, and businesses.

As you start doing your part to resolve the theft, keep detailed records of what you've done and how much you've spent, as your time and money will be among the main things covered in your policy. (The insurance typically doesn't cover direct financial losses from the theft.) Keep receipts and records for phone calls, mileage, legal assistance, notarization, time lost from work, and anything else that is covered.

It Wasn't Me! Warding Off the Debt Collectors

Even after you've taken all the necessary steps to reporting and resolving your identity theft case, your nightmare may not be over. It can take months or sometimes years before your records are completely straightened out. In the meantime, your mailbox may be filling with bills, and your phone ringing off the hook with calls from collection agencies. What to do?

First, send a certified letter to each of the debt collectors informing them that you're a victim of identity theft and that the debts aren't yours. Ask them to send you a copy of any paperwork that supports the debt, such as a loan application or signed service agreement.

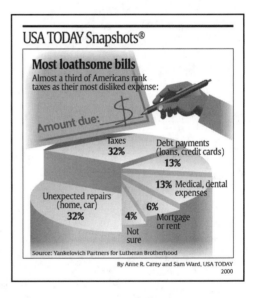

USA TODAY Snapshots®

Most loathsome bills
Almost a third of Americans rank taxes as their most disliked expense:

Amount due:

Taxes **32%**
Debt payments (loans, credit cards) **13%**
13% Medical, dental expenses
Unexpected repairs (home, car) **32%**
6%
4% Mortgage or rent
Not sure

Source: Yankelovich Partners for Lutheran Brotherhood

By Anne R. Carey and Sam Ward, USA TODAY 2000

Once the debt collectors send you the requested paperwork, send follow-up letters to each of them stating that the debts are fraudulent, and requesting that they remove them from your records (different companies may have different steps and forms to clear up identity theft disputes). Your letter should also point out any discrepancies in the paperwork that prove that the debts aren't yours. For example, if they sent you a signed loan application, send them your ID Theft Affidavit, which includes your real signature. You can also point out that the identity thief's street address or birthday doesn't match yours.

Finally, ask that they stop calling you and sending you bills requesting payment for the fraudulent debt. If you notify debt collectors not to contact you, they are legally obligated to cease contact. They can only contact you one more time to explain any action they intend to take. ●

Stay Ahead of the Curve

ongratulations! You've taken the time to learn about identity theft and how you can prevent it, and you're now less likely to be victimized by con artists, or inadvertently put at risk by overzealous marketers, careless clerks, or brainy hackers. Even if your identity is stolen, you now know how to ensure that the least amount of damage will be done.

But to stay ahead of the identity theft curve, you must stay informed. You've already seen how identity thieves keep coming up with new tricks to steal your information, challenging you to stay alert and informed about their latest scams. This chapter offers some valuable information on how you can do that.

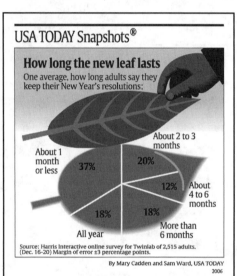

To keep you armed with the latest information, we've created a companion website for this book, www.stoppingidtheft. org. The site includes links to many of the resources discussed in this book, as well as new and updated information on the latest identity theft trends, scams, and news.

Testing Your Identity Theft Savvy

You've learned a lot in the last 11 chapters. Ready to test your knowledge? Select True or False for each of the following questions:

1. It's safe to carry your Social Security card in your purse or wallet.

2. When registering your child for school, it's okay to fill in your child's Social Security number on the application.

3. Preapproved credit card offers are valuable finds for dumpster divers.

4. You can lower the costs of identity theft by ordering your credit report once a year.

5. Your mom's maiden name is a strong password.

6. When shopping on a secure website, you'll see the address bar change from "http" to "https" when you get to the checkout page.

7. You are protected against identity theft on the Internet if you have a firewall and Internet security software to block out intruders, hackers, and criminals.

8. A legitimate company will not ask for personal information in an email message.

9. Elderly people are unlikely targets of identity theft because thieves perceive them as having little or no income.

10. Financial identity theft is the most dangerous type of identity theft.

To determine your score, give yourself one point for each correct answer.

1. **False.** Your Social Security number may be all an identity thief needs to steal your identity. It should be stored in a safe place (think fireproof safe) and taken out only when needed.

2. **False.** You don't need to give out your or your child's Social Security number unless it's required by a government agency, credit bureau, or legitimate U.S.-based financial institution or employer. Schools, medical offices, and other organizations can use alternate means of identification.

3. **True.** If you toss preapproved credit offers in your trash without shredding them, dumpster divers may find them and use them to order credit cards in your name, with the bills going to the thieves' address.

4. **True.** The earliest signs of identity theft are frequently spotted in credit reports. By getting a free credit report at least once a year (or better yet, getting one every four months from one of the big three credit reporting agencies), you can check that everything in your file is accurate.

5. **False.** A strong password uses a combination of letters, numbers, and other characters.

6. **True.** It's important to look for a Web address (URL) that begins with "https://" and the "closed padlock" icon on your browser. You should also enter the address of any banking or e-commerce website in your browser, rather than following a link to it.

7. **False.** Security software is an important first step toward online security, but it doesn't completely protect you from online identity theft. Online attacks can be psychological in nature, luring you into handing over your sensitive information rather than exploiting a software flaw.

8. **True.** Legitimate organizations, such as banks and e-commerce organizations, will never ask you to give out your sensitive information. Be suspicious of any email or phone calls with urgent requests for personal or financial information, such as user names, passwords, credit card numbers, and Social Security numbers.

9. **False.** Thieves frequently target the elderly for several reasons. Many seniors have built up healthy savings and retirement accounts, which are gold mines for identity thieves. In addition, the elderly are less familiar with technology and therefore more likely to fall for online scams.

10. **False.** While financial identity theft can wreak havoc on your credit report and leave you with an empty wallet, medical identity theft can hurt even more. If a thief messes with your medical records, you could end up with an inaccurate medical history.

If you scored a perfect ten, you're ready and well equipped to fight identity thieves. If you scored less than ten, don't worry. Everything you need to know is in this book. You can go back at any time to reread any section.

Keeping Up With the Latest Tricks and Trends

There's no doubt that identity theft is here to stay. And the problem apparently gets worse every year, as the crime evolves and becomes more organized. Many recent frauds share similarities—common addresses, websites, targets, and tactics—that lead law enforcement officials to believe they're being executed by organized and professional crime rings.

So it's no surprise that new and harder-to-detect types of fraud keep cropping up. For example, synthetic identity fraud, in which thieves use pieces of your identity to create a separate and unique identity, is one of the newest and most lucrative twists. The thieves can apply for new accounts in the name of a nonexistent person, with a whole separate billing address, so that, in most cases, the theft goes undetected for years. And you have no right to view the other credit report that contains bits of your information (most likely your Social Security number), as it would violate the privacy of the other person (the identity thief). You'd only find out after the thief defaulted on making payments and you started to get harassing calls from debt collectors, who have tracked you down based on your Social Security number. While creditors and businesses are the primary victims of synthetic identity theft, consumers frequently end up having to prove that they aren't responsible for the fraudulent debts.

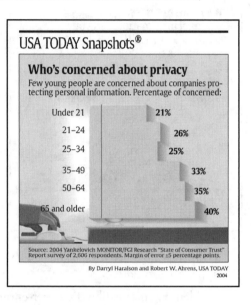

USA TODAY Snapshots®

Who's concerned about privacy
Few young people are concerned about companies protecting personal information. Percentage of concerned:

Under 21	21%
21–24	26%
25–34	25%
35–49	33%
50–64	35%
65 and older	40%

Source: 2004 Yankelovich MONITOR/FGI Research "State of Consumer Trust" Report survey of 2,606 respondents. Margin of error ±5 percentage points.

By Darryl Haralson and Robert W. Ahrens, USA TODAY
2004

In the online world, identity thieves are constantly coming up with new types of malware and scams to trick you into giving out your information. For example, as more and more people become aware of the dangers of phishing emails, scammers add new twists to make them harder to distinguish from the legitimate ones. That's why today's phishing emails are getting much more personal. Phishers know you'll be suspicious of an email that appears to come from eBay or American Express, but what about one that appears to come from your best friend Sam? They use information

USA TODAY Snapshots®

If you are not missing any personal information, can you still be a victim of ID theft?

Percentage that say you can't, by income:

30.5%
13.8%
6.6%
3.0%

Less than $25,000 | $25,000 to $49,000 | $50,000 to $74,000 | More than $74,000

Source: American Express ID theft quiz of 1,007 respondents. Margin of error ±3 percentage points.

By Darryl Haralson and Marcy E. Mullins, USA TODAY 2004

specific to you, figuring that you'll trust the sender if the connection appears legitimate.

"Identity theft is like the never-ending story," said Linda Foley, Identity Theft Resource Center (ITRC) Founder, in a press release. "It acts like an oil spill that spreads in yet another direction with the ocean currents and wind despite best efforts to contain it."

How Paranoid Should You Be?

As Scott McNealy, former CEO of Sun Microsystems, famously said: "You have no privacy, get over it." While we don't recommend using that as an excuse for inaction, we do think it's important to recognize the limits on anyone's control. Our data lives in hundreds of different locations, and is bought and sold hundreds, sometimes thousands of times a year. It's lost by companies we trust on a regular basis, adding up to over 100 million compromised records a year. And we, as individuals, hand our own data out or leave it exposed far too often.

For example, you might complete a credit card application to get a free T-shirt at a baseball game. Sure, you might have every intention of canceling that card; but you've just handed over your personal and financial information to a guy in a sales booth. Similarly, if your husband emails you at work to request your Social Security number to complete your tax return, you might email it back to him, especially if you're too swamped to call. While this is the easiest option at the time, what if his email or Internet connection is compromised by a cybercriminal? Your Social Security number could end up in the wrong hands. This type of carefree behavior leads to millions of Americans falling victim to identity theft every year.

But does this mean we should give up modern conveniences in order to keep our information safe? Absolutely not. Advances in technology have had a profound affect on our lives. You can pay your bills online, research and book the vacation of your dreams in 15 minutes flat, check your email via your BlackBerry while playing hooky from work, and file your taxes from your living room. Who wants to give these up?

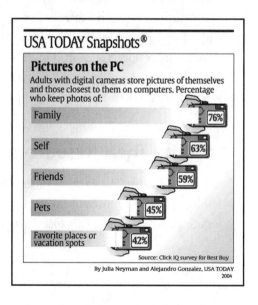

USA TODAY Snapshots®

Pictures on the PC

Adults with digital cameras store pictures of themselves and those closest to them on computers. Percentage who keep photos of:

Family 76%
Self 63%
Friends 59%
Pets 45%
Favorite places or vacation spots 42%

Source: Click IQ survey for Best Buy

By Julia Neyman and Alejandro Gonzalez, USA TODAY 2004

Trading off privacy for convenience is a common decision. You're making this tradeoff when you leave a house key with the next-door neighbors so they can bring in the mail while you're on vacation. You're also making it when you register for an online magazine subscription, which is free in exchange for your personal information.

The truth is that you're at risk whenever you give your information to anybody. It's up to you to decide where to draw the line. Your best bet is to be selective about which companies and individuals you give information to. For example, you'll enjoy discounts by ordering your books from Amazon.com or joining a supermarket "loyalty club," but you'll also surrender information about your buying habits. It's up to you to decide if this tradeoff is worth it.

The key is to take the time to learn how much of a tradeoff you're actually agreeing to. This is where a company's privacy policy comes into play. Will the company reveal all your data to whomever pays it, or does it promise to keep your information secure? Ask these questions before handing over your data. Any worthwhile company will readily direct you to a preprepared statement on the topic.

Finally, by following the steps in this book to protect your identity, home, family, and computers, you've significantly reduced your odds of becoming a victim. You now understand how to safely email, surf the Web, shop, bank, and travel, while protecting your information. You know how thieves can use your Social Security number, credit cards, and other information to steal your identity, and how to prevent them from doing so, or at least find out about it soon after. This means that you can enjoy the conveniences this world has to offer while keeping your identity as safe as it can be.

Identity Theft Resources

Below is a list of the top agencies and websites that can help you prevent, resolve, and learn more about identity theft. This list is regularly updated on our companion website, located at www.stoppingidtheft.org.

Credit Reporting Agencies: Contact to order a free credit report or place a fraud alert or credit freeze.

Equifax	Address: P.O. Box 740241, Atlanta, GA 30374 Website: www.equifax.com Report Fraud: 800-525-6285 Order a Credit Report: 800-685-1111
Experian	Address: P.O. Box 2002, Allen, TX 75013 Website: www.experian.com Report Fraud: 888-EXPERIAN (397-3742) Order a Credit Report: 888-397-3742
TransUnion	Address: P.O. Box 1000, Chester, PA 19022 Website: www.transunion.com Report Fraud: 800-680-7289 Order a Credit Report: 800-916-8800

Federal Government Resources: File a complaint with these agencies if your identity has been stolen. You'll also find information on preventing and resolving identity theft on these websites.

Federal Trade Commission	Address: Identity Theft Clearinghouse, 600 Pennsylvania Avenue, NW, Washington, DC 20580 Website: www.consumer.gov/idtheft Report Fraud: 877-438-4338
Social Security Administration	Address: P.O. Box 17768, Baltimore, MD 21235 Website: www.ssa.gov Report Social Security Fraud: 800-269-0271

Nonprofit Resources: Offer education and assistance for identity theft prevention and resolution.

Identity Theft Resource Center	Address: P.O. Box 26833, San Diego, CA 92196 Website: www.idtheftcenter.org Phone: 858-693-7935
Privacy Rights Clearinghouse	Address: 3100 5th Ave., Suite B, San Diego, CA 92103 Website: www.privacyrights.org Phone: 619-298-3396
Health Privacy Project	Address: 1120 19th St., 8th Floor, Washington, DC 20036 Website: www.healthprivacy.org Phone: 202-721-5632

Medical Records: Request a copy of your medical history file.

Medical Information Bureau	Address: P.O. Box 105, Essex Station, Boston, MA 02112 Website: www.mib.com Request medical record: www.mib.com/html/request_your_record.html Phone: 617-426-3660

Check Fraud Assistance: Get assistance and support in the areas of check fraud, forgery, counterfeiting, bank fraud, and white collar crimes.	
National Check Fraud Center (information on check fraud)	Website: www.ckfraud.org
TeleCheck (place fraud alert on your file)	Website: www.TeleCheck.com
Global Payments Check Services (place fraud alert on your file)	Website: www.globalpaymentsinc.com
Shared Check Authorization Network (place fraud alert on your file)	Phone: 800-262-7771
Consumer Reporting Agencies: Order a consumer file to see what's in your file.	
ChoiceTrust—CLUE Report (insurance reports)	Phone: 866-312-8076
ISO Insurance Services (insurance reports)	Phone: 800-627-3487
ChoicePoint (employment records)	Phone: 866-312-8075
Acxiom (employment records)	Phone: 800-853-3228
ChoicePoint Tenant History (tenant records)	Phone: 877-448-5732
Opt out of marketing lists	
CRA's marketing lists (remove yourself from the lists)	Website: www.optoutprescreen.com Phone: 888-567-8688
Direct Marketing Association's (DMA) Mail Preference Service (opt out of receiving direct mail marketing)	Address: Direct Marketing Association, Mail Preference Service, P.O. Box 643, Carmel, NY 10512 Website: www.dmachoice.org
Federal Trade Commission's Do Not Call registry (opt out of telemarketing calls)	Website: www.donotcall.gov Phone: 888-382-1222

Index

Q

R

S

Get the Latest in the Law

Nolo's Legal Updater
We'll send you an email whenever a new edition of your book is published! Sign up at **www.nolo.com/legalupdater**.

Updates at Nolo.com
Check **www.nolo.com/update** to find recent changes in the law that affect the current edition of your book.

Nolo Customer Service
To make sure that this edition of the book is the most recent one, call us at **800-728-3555** and ask one of our friendly customer service representatives (7:00 am to 6:00 pm PST, weekdays only). Or find out at **www.nolo.com**.

Complete the Registration & Comment Card ...
... and we'll do the work for you! Just indicate your preferences below:

NOLO *and* USA TODAY

Cutting-Edge Content, Unparalleled Expertise

The Busy Family's Guide to Money
by Sandra Block, Kathy Chu & John Waggoner

Drawing on the experience of three respected USA TODAY financial writers, *The Busy Family's Guide to Money* will help you make the most of your income, handle major one-time expenses, figure children into the budget—and much more. **$19.99**

The Work From Home Handbook
Flex Your Time, Improve Your Life
by Diana Fitzpatrick & Stephen Fishman

If you're one of those people who need to (or simply want to) work from home, let this concise and powerful book help you come up with a plan that both you and your boss can embrace! **$19.99**

Retire Happy
What You Can Do NOW to Guarantee a Great Retirement
by Richard Stim & Ralph Warner

You don't need a million dollars to retire well, but you do need friends, hobbies and an active lifestyle. This book covers all the financial and personal necessities that can make retirement the best time of your life. **$19.99**

Easy Ways to Lower Your Taxes
Simple Strategies Every Taxpayer Should Know
by Sandra Block & Stephen Fishman

Provides useful insights and tactics to help lower your taxes. Learn how to boost tax-free income, get a lower tax rate, defer paying taxes, make the most of deductions—and more! **$19.99**

First-Time Landlord
Your Guide to Renting Out a Single-Family Home
by Attorney Janet Portman, Marcia Stewart & Michael Molinski

From choosing tenants to handling repairs to avoiding legal trouble, *First-Time Landlord* provides the information new landlords need to be effective, make a profit and follow the law. **$19.99**